GHOST FIELDS OF NORFOLK

About the Author: Officially dubbed an anorak by the Eastern Daily Press, Rod McKenzie pursues an obsessive interest in all aspects of aviation, with a particular emphasis on the aerial conflicts of World War 2. In researching this project he has travelled all over Norfolk – mainly by bicycle – and taken hundreds of photographs. He lives quietly in North Wootton with his wife Carolyn, and for his sins follows the Pittsburgh Steelers.

Ghost Fields of Norfolk

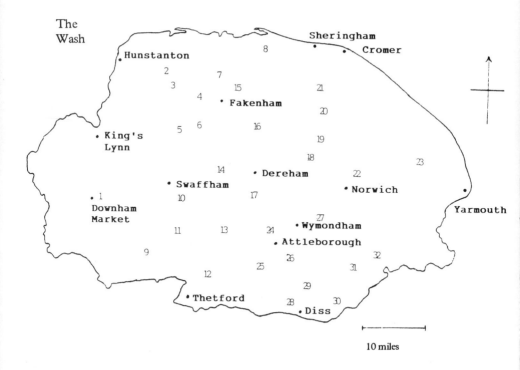

Key:

1. Downham Market
2. Docking
3. Bircham Newton
4. Sculthorpe
5. Great Massingham
6. West Raynham
7. North Creake
8. Langham
9. Methwold
10. North Pickenham
11. Bodney
12. East Wretham
13. Watton
14. Wendling
15. Little Snoring
16. Foulsham
17. Shipdham
18. Attlebridge
19. Swannington
20. Oulton
21. Matlask
22. Rackheath
23. Ludham
24. Deopham Green
25. Snetterton Heath
26. Old Buckenham
27. Hethel
28. Fersfield
29. Tibenham
30. Thorpe Abbotts
31. Hardwick
32. Seething

Ghost Fields of Norfolk

*History, plans and photographed remains
of 32 Norfolk airfields*

Roderick McKenzie

Respectfully dedicated to the Coach himself

Hugh Rose McKenzie

- who didn't think it was such a crazy idea

Larks Press

Published by the Larks Press
Ordnance Farmhouse, Guist Bottom, Dereham,
Norfolk NR20 5PF
01328 829207
Larks.Press@btinternet.com
Website: www.booksatlarkspress.co.uk

Printed February 2004 and reprinted
2004, 2005, 2007 by the Lanceni Press

Reprinted 2010, 2013 by Newprint and Design Ltd
Garrood Drive, Fakenham, Norfolk

British Library Cataloguing-in-Publication Data
A catalogue record for this book is available
from the British Library

Front cover: Sunset at Great Massingham airfield

Acknowledgements

This project has been greatly assisted by the co-operation of the following individuals and organisations:

Mr R.G.Armsby; Mike Baxter; O.C.Brun Esq.; Johanna Cook (Ordnance Survey); Jakki Daley (Dalgety); John Edwards (RAF Museum); Mr Elyard; Sid English; Pauline Fisher; John Freeman (Defence Estates – West Tofts); Mrs C. Gibbons (Defence Estates – Waterbeach); Doug Parnham; Andrea Pawley (National Construction College); Mr Philpott; Mr E.R.P.Pratt; Joanne Ratcliffe (RAF Museum); Ian Reid (FPD Savills); David Store (Ordnance Survey); Sunderland Farm (Docking); Tinker Taylor; Mr T. Webster (RMC Aggregates).

Thanks to Mr and Mrs Beales of Hill Farm, Great Ellingham, for their hospitality.

Special thanks to Len Bartram, an unfailing source of encouragement and information.

ISBN 978 1 904006 17 6

Foreword

This project had its genesis during the wretched summer of 1998. On one of the very few fine days, my wife and I cycled over to Great Massingham and, knowing that this was the site of a (still active) World War 2 airfield, we took some time to explore. There wasn't much to see, but an idea had been planted.

In October I dragged my long-suffering parents on a one-day six-airfield tour of North Norfolk. Two sites in particular, Langham and North Creake, fired my imagination, seeming to me almost perfectly preserved time capsules, loaded with atmosphere. As autumn fringed into winter I was able to add the mysterious site at Docking and the legendary Bircham Newton to my list, and over the Christmas period, when I was fortunate enough to be on holiday in Texas, my thoughts crystallised into a definite project, the result of which you now hold in your hands.

The emphasis of this book is not primarily historical: Norfolk's rich aviation heritage has been thoroughly documented already, and those seeking more detailed information are directed to the works listed in the bibliography. Rather, the historical outlines presented here provide a context for the the photographs and plans, which record what can still be discovered at these often remote locations. Hopefully, the photographs give at least a taste of the powerfully evocative atmosphere that pervades these places, a feeling that only intensifies with a working knowledge of the remarkable events that unfolded at each and every one of them.

My wife has commented that this book is essentially a collection of photographs of fields, and it is a fair point: those hoping for glimpses of Norfolk's often splendid scenery are likely to be disappointed. But there can be no better places to appreciate the gorgeous skies for which East Anglia is justly celebrated, and, as students of Agincourt, Bosworth and Flanders will tell you, some fields are more significant than others.

Roderick McKenzie
North Wootton, January 2004.

Bibliography

Bartram, Len - *RAF Docking & Bircham Newton* (Privately published)
Bartram, Len - *RAF Foulsham 1942-54* (Privately published)
Bartram, Len - *RAF Langham 1940-58* (Privately published)
Bartram, Len - *RAF Matlaske 1940-45* (Privately published)
Bartram, Len - *RAF North Creake 1940-47* (Privately published)
Bartram, Len - *RAF Oulton 1940-47* (Privately published)
Bowyer, Michael J.F. - *Action Stations 1: East Anglia* (PSL) 1990
Congdon, Philip - *Behind the Hangar Doors* (Sonik)
Fairhead, Huby - *Decoy Sites* (Norfolk & Suffolk Aviation Museum)
Fairhead, Huby & Tuffen, Roy - *Airfields & Airstrips of Norfolk & Suffolk* (Norfolk & Suffolk Aviation Museum)
Francis, Paul - *Military Airfield Architecture* (PSL) 1996
Freeman, Roger - *Airfields of the Eighth Then and Now* (After the Battle) 1978
Freeman, Roger - *The Mighty Eighth in Colour* (Arms & Armour) 1991
Freeman, Roger - *The Royal Air Force of World War Two in Colour* (Arms & Armour) 1993
Gunn, Peter B. - *Airfield Focus 5: Bircham Newton* (GMS) 1992
Gunston, Bill - *Aircraft of World War 2* (St Michael) 1981
Hilling, John B. - *Strike Hard - A Bomber Airfield at War* (Sutton) 1995
Innes, Graham Buchan - *British Airfield Buildings of the Second World War* (Midland) 1995
Innes, Graham Buchan - *British Airfield Buildings - Expansion & Inter-War Periods* (Midland) 2000
Jefford, Wg Cdr C.J. - *RAF Squadrons* (Airlife) 1988
McLachlan, Ian - *Final Flights* (PSL)
McLachlan, Ian & Zorn, Russell J. - *Eighth Air Force Bomber Stories* (PSL)
Narborough Airfield Research Group - *The Great Government Aerodrome* (Privately published) 2000
Smith, Graham - *Norfolk Airfields in the Second World War* (Countryside) 1994
Walker, Peter M. - *Norfolk Military Airfields* (Privately published) 1997

Introduction

At the close of the Second World War, the County of Norfolk played host to no less than thirty-seven major military airfields. Of these, only two – RAF Coltishall and RAF Marham – survive as frontline operational stations. Feltwell, although no longer used for flying, maintains a vital strategic role as an air/space tracking station supporting the Lakenheath-based USAF 'Liberty Wing'. The former American bomber base of Horsham St Faith has been transmogrified into the thriving commercial concern that is Norwich Airport, and thus falls outside the scope of this volume. So too does Swanton Morley, which maintains a schizoid existence: the north side, including the magnificent all-grass flying field, is now an army barracks; the south side, complete with historic T2 hangar, is a haven for light aviation best known for its superb Boeing Stearman biplane restorations.

The remaining 32 airfields form the primary focus of this survey, and several of these remain Ministry of Defence property. Bodney, East Wretham, Sculthorpe and Watton are all linked to the massive live-firing Stanford Training Area, although only parts of these sites are retained by the military. West Raynham – one of the most historic airfields in the country – stands perfectly mothballed but facing an uncertain future.

Meanwhile light aviation flourishes at many Norfolk locations. Great Massingham, Hardwick, Langham, Little Snoring, Ludham, Old Buckenham, Seething, Shipdham & Tibenham all see private flying to a greater or lesser degree, with activities ranging from simple crop-dusting to national-level aerobatics and gliding competitions. Skies that throughout the week reverberate to the roar of RAF Jaguars and Tornados give way at weekends to droning swarms of Cessnas and Pipers, Beeches and Jodels, especially during the summer months.

The remainder of the sites are derelict in aviation and military terms, yet these are probably the most evocative locations in this book. Some, such as Downham Market, have been so badly mauled in the modern era that they are barely recognisable; others, like Bircham Newton, are in such a pristine state that they still feel like operational stations. In an interesting sidebar, both Hethel and Snetterton Heath now have deep-rooted associations with very fast motor cars, but generally such locations have passed into either agricultural or industrial usage, and frequently both.

As a rule of thumb, derelict airfields can be divided into sites where runways and taxiways have survived (e.g. Attlebridge), and those where a large number of buildings still stand (e.g. North Creake). It is comparatively rare to find locations that meet both criteria. At sites that have returned to agriculture, runways and perimeter tracks are usually reduced to tractor width, but occasional full-size sections remain, and can take the breath away with their sheer scale. Of the buildings that survive, by far the most inspiring

1

are the Control Towers (Watch Offices in wartime RAF parlance), and it is no surprise that two of these have become museums, with the possibility of more to follow. Next in order of precedence, and surprisingly numerous, are the Operations Blocks, closely followed by the structures that most obviously denote the former presence of aircraft – hangars.

The imposing, brick-faced C-type hangars seen at Bircham, Raynham and Watton are symbolic of the 1930s RAF expansion (see below). The fact that these huge buildings have been an accepted part of the landscape of Norfolk (and elsewhere) for over 60 years speaks volumes for their design, which took into account contemporary public opinion. However, with the outbreak of war, a need was quickly identified for portable hangars that could be mass-produced and quickly erected at the airfields that were springing up all over the country. These were the T – (for transportable) type hangars, of which the T2 was by far the most numerous, with over 900 being produced, and today this is still the most ubiquitous type at airfields both operational and derelict. Indeed such is the usefulness of the T2 that a number have been re-erected at locations where no airfield ever existed, which can confuse the casual observer.

It needs to be borne in mind that the T2s were never intended to have any sort of permanence. In fact, none of the buildings at airfields constructed during World War 2 – and this includes those of brick-faced concrete – were designed to last more than ten years. The fact that so many have survived, when in all but a few cases no attempt has been made to preserve or even maintain them, is a testament to their design and durability of construction.

That old cliché – 'very flat, Norfolk' – has achieved wide currency, but those who subscribe to it have obviously never attempted to cycle round the place. In fact, Norfolk is only flat at its eastern and western extremities; to the west lies the wide-open fenland, and to the east the vast wetland areas known as the Broads. In between, the landscape, while it could not be called hilly, undulates consistently; and the presence of large, level, well-drained patches of higher ground made it eminently desirable for the building of airfields.

The Royal Air Force came into existence on 1st April 1918, formed from the merger of the Royal Flying Corps and the Royal Naval Air Service. However, with the end of the First World War the fledgling service imploded from around 180 squadrons to just 29 by March 1920. Hand-in-hand with this, was a marked decline in the number of ærodromes – in Norfolk such major concerns as Narborough and Sedgeford very rapidly became derelict.

Not until the mid-1930s, with an increasingly uncertain situation in Continental Europe, did the RAF embark on a serious expansion. The initial phase, in 1935, included the construction of Feltwell and the development of the hitherto minor World War 1 station at Marham. Successive expansion programmes saw the development of Bircham Newton and the building of permanent stations at Coltishall, Horsham St Faith, Swanton Morley, Watton and West Raynham. Thus it was that the RAF, in Norfolk as elsewhere, was just ready for the outbreak of war in 1939. But this rate of growth was chickenfeed compared to the explosion of airfield building that occurred once hostilities had begun.

Between 1939-1945, no less than 444 airfields were constructed in the British Isles, at a cost of over £200 million. At the peak, in 1942, a new airfield was being opened every three days. Many of these were Class A bomber airfields, with three concrete runways – usually a 2,000-yard main, plus two 1,400-yard subsidiaries in a triangular layout – and concrete perimeter track, taxiways and anything up to fifty dispersals of either the 'frying pan' or 'loop' types.

During this programme, some lessons, hard-earned during the early years of conflict, were put into practice. The expansion-era sites were notable for their concentration of facilities – hangars, technical site and accommodation blocks were situated within easy walking distance of each other. This no doubt made sense from an operational standpoint, but inevitably it made these locations highly vulnerable to enemy attack. Later airfields were marked by wide dispersal of facilities all around the site, with such elements as bomb dumps often being concealed in nearby woodland. With accommodation sites this was taken to extremes, and these could be located up to three miles from the actual flying field. Many of these dispersed sites survive, and are worthy of study in their own right, but are not a focus of this volume. Dispersed sites are only featured if they are of particular interest, or in the immediate vicinity of the main airfield site.

The effort involved in such a construction programme beggars the modern imagination: to take a single example, the site at Rackheath, near Norwich, involved excavating 556,000 cubic yards of soil and the laying of 504,000 cubic yards of concrete. The perimeter track alone was over 2½ miles long. Rackheath was one of the airfields built specifically for the Americans, who began operating from UK soil in 1942 and rapidly built up an awesome ærial armada mainly comprised of bomber and fighter units of the Eighth Air Force, an organisation whose exploits are today the stuff of legend.

The Americans were heavily represented in Norfolk, although it was neighbouring Suffolk that would eventually earn the soubriquet of 'Little America'. However, Norfolk could additionally boast the presence of all three major RAF Commands – Bomber, Fighter and Coastal – making its wartime ærial history a near-perfect microcosm of the entire European air war.

If any one element could be said to connect the sites surveyed in this volume, it is silence. Sculthorpe and Watton are capable of frenetic activity during exercises, but most of the time they are peaceful save for the skylarks and the keening of the wind. The locations that survive as private ærodromes are literally abuzz during summer weekends, but at other times there is no sound and often no movement. Those sites that have slipped into purely agricultural usage are empty wildernesses, apart from the occasional echoing growl of a tractor or combine harvester; meanwhile the busy industrial estates become soundless mausoleums at weekends.

It is in these silences that a farm becomes once more a runway from which mighty bombers lifted; that a small industrial unit reverts to being a busy Mess Hall; that a metal-walled grain store is again filled with the silhouettes of extinct military aircraft. In these silences, the ghosts walk once more upon the Ghost Fields.

Attlebridge features some of the best-preserved runways in Norfolk, all of which are visible in this view looking from the SE corner of the site. The perimeter track splits from the NW-SE runway just beyond the present gates; the poultry shed on the left is built on the NE-SW runway; while those visible in the centre-left and right background occupy the E-W main, thus completing the classic A pattern.

4

Attlebridge

Attlebridge opened in July 1941 as a satellite of the major Bomber Command station at Swanton Morley. In what would become a familiar pattern at Second World War Norfolk airfields, its first occupants were Bristol Blenheims of 105 Squadron, dispersed from the parent station. Evolved from an executive transport design, the Blenheim was cutting-edge when it entered RAF service in 1937, but the rapid pace of development stimulated by war soon left it behind.

88 Squadron – also flying Blenheims – was the first unit to be properly based at Attlebridge, and they conducted a variety of daring and harrowing low-level missions against enemy ports and shipping. They converted to the Douglas Boston before going on to even greater feats operating from other airfields.

A very unusual unit appeared briefly at Attlebridge in the autumn of 1942. The 319th Bomb Group was part of the American 12th Air Force, operating the formidable – and rather notorious – Martin Marauder. They conducted no missions from Norfolk, but continued working up for eventual deployment to North Africa. Unfortunately, some Marauders were lost on training flights.

In its early years Attlebridge was generally under-used, and it closed in the autumn of 1943. However, this was merely to facilitate the second phase in its history, as the site had been assigned to the USAAF 8th Air Force, becoming Station 120. Concrete runways and dispersals were laid as the field was upgraded to heavy bomber status. It re-opened in 1944 to host the 466th Bomb Group, flying another aircraft type that was to become synonymous with Norfolk skies: the Consolidated B24 Liberator. Subject of one of the most costly development programmes in aviation history, the B24 was produced in greater quantity than any other American bomber, over 19,000 eventually being built.

First mission for the 466th was on 22nd March 1944, to the biggest target of them all – Berlin. The Group went on to conduct 232 operations, including the vital ferrying of fuel to forward bases in France in September 1944. Over all, their loss rate compared favourably with other Bomb Groups, their worst day being 14th May when six B24s were lost on a mission to Brunswick. Their final operation was carried out on 25th April 1945, and by July the Group had returned to the States.

Attlebridge was sold off in March 1959, and for many years has been a turkey farm, part of the famous Bernard Matthews operation. Despite this, much remains to be seen, and is easily viewed as several public roads between Hockering and Weston Longville encircle the site.

Attlebridge – Operational History

Unit	Aircraft Type	Resident	Role
88 sqn	Blenheim IV Boston III	Aug. 41 – Sept. 41	Light bombing
319th BG (US 12th AF) 437th, 438th Bomb sqns	B26C Marauder	Oct. 42 – Nov. 42	Medium bombing
320 sqn	Mitchell II	Mar 43 – Aug. 43	Light bombing
1508 BAT Flt	Oxford I	Apr. 43 – Aug. 43	Blind approach training
247 sqn	Typhoon Ib	Aug. 43	Fighter
466th BG (US 8th AF) 784th, 785th, 786th, 787th Bomb sqns	B24H, J, L, M Liberator	Mar 44 – July 45	Heavy day bombing

Note: 247 sqn's brief deployment to this bomber station was in response to a spate of Luftwaffe attacks on the East Anglian coast – a threat that receded almost as soon as it began.

Attlebridge Plan

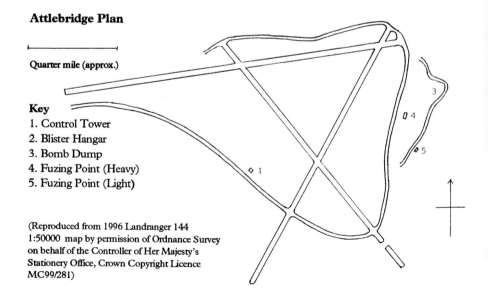

Quarter mile (approx.)

Key
1. Control Tower
2. Blister Hangar
3. Bomb Dump
4. Fuzing Point (Heavy)
5. Fuzing Point (Light)

(Reproduced from 1996 Landranger 144
1:50000 map by permission of Ordnance Survey
on behalf of the Controller of Her Majesty's
Stationery Office, Crown Copyright Licence
MC99/281)

A view of the bomb dump, with its taxiway curving northwards and a fuzing point (light) lurking beyond the blast banking.

This blister hangar is one of the most significant buildings surviving on site.

Attlebridge : The view east along the extended main runway.

Bircham Newton

For the student of military airfield architecture, Bircham Newton is a motherlode. With a history stretching back to the First World War, its buildings chart a continuous line of development through to closure as an operational station in 1962, including the so-called 'Expansion Period' of the mid-to-late 1930s. During the Second World War, as the hub of coastal command's operations on the east coast, Bircham generated so much traffic that it spawned two satellite fields, at Docking and Langham.

The site first opened as an airfield in 1916; however it was not until after the formation of the Royal Air Force in April 1918 that work began in earnest to develop an operational ærodrome. After a brief period of use for fighter training, in June 1918 it began an association with bomber aircraft that lasted until 1936. In that year the station was transferred to Coastal Command, and underwent a major redevelopment that resulted in most of the buildings still standing today, in particular the C-type hangars that dominate the surrounding landscape.

From the outbreak of hostilities through to the end of World War 2, Bircham played host to an astonishing variety of units and aircraft, as listed below. Throughout it remained an all-grass airfield, although steel matting was laid to accommodate heavier types such as Warwicks, Wellingtons and Whitleys.

Post-war, flying activities at Bircham dwindled as the station was transferred, first to Flying Training Command, then to Transport Command, and finally to Technical Training Command, under whose auspices it saw out its final years as an officers' school. Officially closed in 1962, the site was sold off in November 1964. However, the station briefly returned to life in 1965, when it was used for trials of the Hawker Siddeley Kestrel VTOL aircraft, forerunner of the legendary Harrier.

Since 1966 Bircham has been home to the National Construction College (formerly the Construction Industry Training Board), and used to teach such skills as building, crane-driving, scaffolding and steeple-jacking. This has meant mixed fortunes for the site. On the plus side, virtually all the major buildings remain intact, and the place still retains the feel of a busy operational station. By contrast, the flying field has suffered badly under the onslaught of dump-trucks and excavators, little remaining except for traces of the perimeter track. Although situated on a public road, the site is strictly private, and anyone wishing to visit **must** obtain prior permission. However, if you content yourself with distant views, there are many points in the surrounding countryside offering vistas of this legendary field.

Bircham Newton – Operational History

Unit	Aircraft Type	Resident	Role
No 3 Fighting School	DH4, DH5, DH9, Avro 504 Bristol M1, Camel, Dolphin, Pup, Snipe, Sopwith Triplane	Apr 18-Nov 18	Fighter tactics training
166 sqn	FE2b, HP 0/400, HP V/1500	Jun 18–May 19	Heavy night bombing
167 sqn	HP V/1500	Nov 18–May 19	Heavy night bombing
274 sqn	HP V/1500	Jun 19–Jan 20	Heavy night bombing
56 sqn	SE5a	Dec 19–Jan 20	Fighter sqn
60 sqn	SE5a	Dec 19–Jan 20	Fighter sqn
207 sqn	DH9a	Feb 20–Sep 22	Day bombing
7 sqn	Vimy, Virginia	Jun 23–Apr 27	Heavy bombing
11 sqn	DH9a, Fawn	Sep 23–May 24	Day bombing
99 sqn	Vimy, Aldershot Hyderabad	May 24–Jan 28	Heavy day bombing
32 sqn	Snipe	Jun 27–Aug 27	Fighter sqn (Exercises)
39 sqn	DH9a	Jan 28–Dec 28	Day bombing
101 sqn	DH9a, Sidestrand III	Mar 28–Oct 29	Day bombing
35 sqn	Fairey IIIF, Gordon	Mar 29–Oct 35	Day bombing
207 sqn	Fairey IIIF, Gordon	Nov 29–Oct 35	Day bombing
48 sqn (B flt)	Cloud	Feb 35–Jan 36	Coastal training Amphibious
21 sqn	Hind	Dec 35–Jul 36	Day bombing
34 sqn	Hind	Dec 35–Jul 36	Day bombing
18 sqn	Hart, Hind	Jan 36–Sep 36	Day bombing
49 sqn	Hind	Jan 36–Sep 36	Day bombing
206 sqn	Anson GR.I Hudson I, II, III, IV	Jun 36–Jul 41	Coastal patrol
269 sqn	Anson GR.I	Jul 36–Dec 39	Coastal patrol
220 sqn	Anson GR.I	Aug 36–Aug 39	Coastal patrol
No 1 AACU (C&D flts)	Wallace II Henley TT.III	May 38-Aug 38 May 39–Aug 39	Target towing Target towing
233 sqn	Anson GR.I	Jun 39–Sep 39	Coastal reconnaissance
42 sqn	Vildebeest III, IV Beaufort GR.I	Aug 39–Apr 40	Torpedo bombing

612 sqn	Anson GR.I	Sep 39–Nov 40	Coastal reconnaissance
233 sqn	Hudson GR.I	Oct 39–Dec 39	Reconnaissance/
	Blenheim IV		Anti-shipping
600 sqn	Blenheim If, IVf	Dec 39	Trade defence
254 sqn	Blenheim If, IVf	Jan 40–Apr 40	Trade defence
815 sqn (RN)	Swordfish I	Apr 40–May 40	Night mine-laying
No 2 GRU	Wellington DW.I	Apr 40–May 40	Anti-mine operations
235 sqn	Blenheim If, IVf	Apr 40–Jun 41	Anti-shipping/
			Convoy defence
826 sqn	Albacore I	May 40-Oct 40	Night shipping patrols
			Mine-laying
812 sqn	Swordfish I	May 40–Jun 40	Mine-laying
229 sqn	Hurricane I	Jun 40–Sep 40	Fighter sqn
No 1 AACU	Henley TT. III	Sep 40–Dec 41	Target towing
(K & M Flts)			
221 sqn	Wellington Ic	Nov 40-May 41	Long range
			anti-shipping
252 sqn	Blenheim Ic, IVf	Nov 40-Dec 40	Trade defence
1403 Met flt	Blenheim I	Nov 40–Jul 42	Weather
	Hudson III		reconnaissance
1401 Met flt	Gladiator II	Mar 41-Aug 43	Weather recon-
			naissance (local)
59 sqn	Blenheim IV	Mar 41-Jun 41	Coastal recon-
			naissance/anti-shipping
500 sqn	Blenheim IV	Apr 41–Apr 42	Coastal recon-
	Hudson V		naissance/anti-shipping
200 sqn	Hudson IV	May 41–Jun 41	Anti-submarine/convoy
			patrol
608 sqn	Blenheim I, IV	Jun 41–Dec 41	Anti-shipping patrol
	Hudson V		
248 sqn	Beaufighter Ic	Jun 41–Feb 42	Anti-shipping
53 sqn	Blenheim IV	Jul 41–Oct 41	Anti-shipping patrol
	Hudson V		
279 sqn	Hudson III, V, VI	Nov 41–Oct 44	Air-sea rescue
407 sqn (RCAF)	Hudson III, V	Mar 42–Nov 42	Anti-shipping patrol
320 sqn	Hudson I, III, V, VI	Apr 42–Mar 43	Shipping strikes/recon.
235 sqn (det)	Beaufighter Ic, VIc	May 42–Jan 43	Strike/convoy
			protection
812 sqn(RN)	Swordfish I	Jul 42–Aug 42	Anti-submarine
811 sqn	Swordfish II	Aug 42–Oct 42	Mine-laying

521 sqn	Mosquito PR. I, IV Spitfire V, Gladiator II Hudson III Blenheim IV Gladiator II	Aug 42–Apr 43	Weather reconnaissance
1611/1612 TT flts	Henley TT.III	Nov 42-Dec 43	Target towing
280 sqn	Anson ASR.I	Nov 42–Sep 43	Air-sea rescue
409 sqn (RCAF)	Beaufighter VIf Mosquito XIII	Feb 43–May 44	Night-fighter sqn
Warwick TU	Warwick	Jul 43–Nov 43	Air-sea rescue training
415 sqn (RCAF)	Wellington GR.XIII Albacore I	Oct 43–Jul 44	Anti-submarine
695 sqn	Henley III Martinet I Vengeance IV Hurricane IIc Lysander I,II Spitfire Vb	Dec 43–Jul 45	Anti-aircraft cooperation
524 sqn	Wellington GR.XIII	Jul 44–Nov 44	Long-range anti- submarine
Coastal Cmd Prep Pool	Various types	Jul 44–May 45	Aircraft mods/servicing
855 sqn (RN)	Avenger II	Sep 44–Oct 44	Anti-shipping strike
119 sqn	Albacore I Swordfish III	Oct 44-May 45	Night anti-shipping
819 sqn	Albacore I Swordfish II	Oct 44–Jan 45	Anti-submarine
598 sqn	Oxford I, II Martinet Hurricane II, IV Beaufighter I	Mar 45–Apr 45	Target towing
1510 ABST flt	Oxford I Anson I	May 45-Sep 48	Beam approach training
Transport Cmd ICU	Oxford T2	Oct 46–Oct 48	Twin-engine conversion
1555 Radio Aids Training flt	Oxford T2	Mar 47-Oct 48	Radio operator training
1559 Radio Aids Training flt	Oxford T2	Mar 47-Oct 48	Radio operator training

Notes

Of the myriad aircraft to operate from Bircham, by far the most intriguing was the Wellington DW.I, as operated by no.2 GRU. This ultra-secret variant of the famous 'Wimpey' was fitted with a giant circular electromagnet, powered by a Ford V8 motor engine mounted in the fusilage. It was intended to combat the new (in 1940) menace of German magnetic mines, the idea being that the low-flying aircraft could safely detonate them by impersonating the magnetic 'signature' of a ship. In practice the device was largely unsuccessful, and the development of alternative counter-measures by the Royal Navy soon rendered these bizarre aircraft redundant.

Trade defence, as conducted by a number of Blenheim squadrons from Bircham, involved the protection of the herring fleets operating in large numbers from the east coast, primarily Great Yarmouth and Lowestoft.

Beautifully preserved, Bircham Newton's watch office is the classic inter-war 'fort' type, to air ministry drawing no. 1959 of 1934.

Bircham Newton Plan

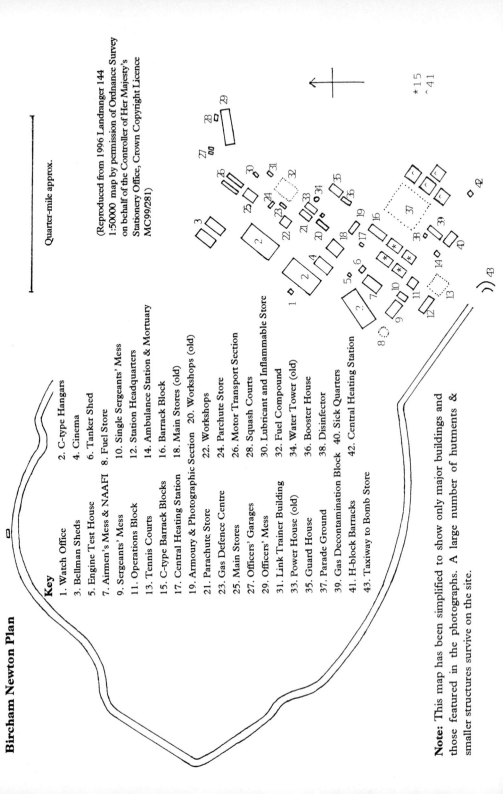

Quarter-mile approx.

(Reproduced from 1996 Landranger 144 1:50000 map by permission of Ordnance Survey on behalf of the Controller of Her Majesty's Stationery Office, Crown Copyright Licence MC99/281)

Key

1. Watch Office
2. C-type Hangars
3. Bellman Sheds
4. Cinema
5. Engine Test House
6. Tanker Shed
7. Airmen's Mess & NAAFI
8. Fuel Store
9. Sergeants' Mess
10. Single Sergeants' Mess
11. Operations Block
12. Station Headquarters
13. Tennis Courts
14. Ambulance Station & Mortuary
15. C-type Barrack Blocks
16. Barrack Block
17. Central Heating Station
18. Main Stores (old)
19. Armoury & Photographic Section
20. Workshops (old)
21. Parachute Store
22. Workshops
23. Gas Defence Centre
24. Parachute Store
25. Main Stores
26. Motor Transport Section
27. Officers' Garages
28. Squash Courts
29. Officers' Mess
30. Lubricant and Inflammable Store
31. Link Trainer Building
32. Fuel Compound
33. Power House (old)
34. Water Tower (old)
35. Guard House
36. Booster House
37. Parade Ground
38. Disinfector
39. Gas Decontamination Block
40. Sick Quarters
41. H-block Barracks
42. Central Heating Station
43. Taxiway to Bomb Store

Note: This map has been simplified to show only major buildings and those featured in the photographs. A large number of hutments & smaller structures survive on the site.

A type C barrack block, to drawing 1100 of 1928.

The infamous squash courts, long reputed to be haunted, are among the oldest buildings at Bircham, being to drawing 2078 of 1918.

Precautions against chemical warfare were a major feature of many airfields. This gas decontamination block is to drawing 6224 of 1937.

Bircham's armoury (left) and photographic section, to drawing 7616, 1937.

Built to drawing 1967 of 1934, the lubricant and inflammables store still fulfills its original role.

A link trainer building, to drawing 6959 of 1938. The link trainer was an early type of simulator, used to teach rudimentary flying skills.

Two of Bircham's older buildings are this high level water tank (left) and the power house, both dating from the 1920s.

The attractive guard house, to drawing 166 of 1923, now has a rather more mundane function.

This is one of two central heating stations at Bircham, to drawing 5710 of 1937.

The main stores, to a 1928 design, were superseded in the expansion era development. Visible beyond is the cinema, converted from the former workshops.

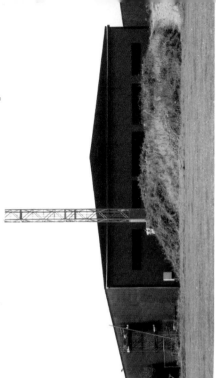

Bircham's operations block, to drawing 7040 of 1938, now serves as NCC's reception centre.

Rare survivor in Norfolk, a Bellman aircraft shed to drawing 2773 of 1934 - one of two still standing at Bircham.

Bodney

One of the most rustic of all-grass airfields, Bodney opened in 1940 as a satellite of Watton. Throughout its early years Watton-based Blenheim squadrons such as 21 and 82 routinely dispersed there and often conducted their difficult and dangerous daylight operations from the site. In May 1941 the peripatetic 90 sqn briefly stopped at Bodney with its experimental B17 Fortresses, but operating heavy bombers from the undeveloped field was a non-starter. 21 sqn returned in 1942 to re-equip with Venturas before moving to Methwold, but generally the airfield was underused.

This all changed in the summer of 1943 when Bodney was transferred to the USAAF, becoming Station 141. The site underwent some expansion and pressed steel matting was laid on the runways and taxiways in order to accommodate the P47 Thunderbolts of the 352nd Fighter Group. Primarily tasked with long-range escort of 8th AF bomber formations, the 352nd also graduated to ground attack and strafing missions. By April 1944 they had exchanged their 'Jugs' for the legendary P51 Mustang.

On 8th May, the 352nd escorted a B24 Liberator force to Brunswick, in the process taking on a huge mixed Luftwaffe force of Fw190s and Bf109s. In the frantic combat that followed, the Group claimed 27 aircraft destroyed against just one loss, receiving a Distinguished Unit Citation for this action. The most famous of several 352nd FG aces was Major George Preddy, who at one point was the 8th AF's highest-scoring fighter pilot with 27 'kills'. With tragic irony, Preddy was shot down and killed by 'friendly fire' over Belgium on Xmas Day, 1944.

The most infamous incident in Bodney's history occurred on one of the most significant dates in human history: June 6th, 1944 – D-Day. Taking off in dreadfully poor visibility, Lieutenant Frascotti's P51 struck the Control Tower, instantly killing the pilot. As a result, a new tower was built on the opposite side of the field, and it is this later structure that survives today.

Bodney closed as an airfield in November 1945 and returned to agriculture – years of neglect have taken their toll and most of the buildings are in an advanced state of ruin. However, the site maintains a quasi-military existence, being part of the Stanford Training Area. Bodney Camp, the former accommodation site dispersed to the south, is still extensively used by the Army. Although off-limits to the public, the field is easily viewed from the B1108 between Bodney village and Watton.

Bodney – Operational History

Unit	Aircraft Type	Resident	Role
21 sqn	Blenheim	Mar 40–Jun 40	Daylight bombing
82 sqn	Blenheim	Mar 40-Apr 41	Daylight bombing
61 sqn	Hampden	Apr 41	Daylight bombing
90 sqn	Fortress I (B17c)	May 41	Heavy bomber trials
105 sqn	Blenheim IV	May 41–Jul 41	Daylight bombing
21 sqn	Blenheim IV Ventura I, II	Mar 42-Oct 42	Light bombing
17 (Pilots) ATU	Master	Sep 42–May 43	Advanced pilot training
352nd FG (US 8thAF) 328th, 486th, 487th Fighter sqns	P47D Thunderbolt P51B,C,D,K Mustang	Jun 43–Feb 45 Apr 45-Nov 45	Bomber escort/Ground attack

L-R: Bodney's control tower, NFE store and tractor shed still keep watch over quasi-military activity, being on the fringes of the Stanford training area.

19

Bodney Plan

Quarter-mile approx.

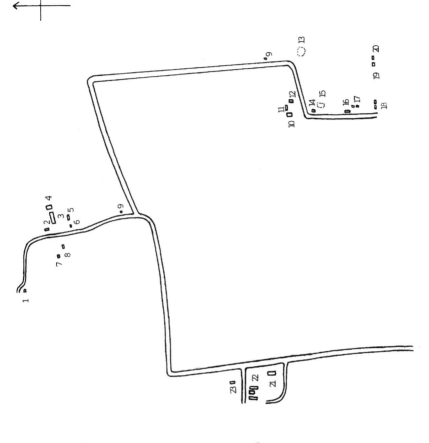

Key

1. Picket Post
2. Rations Store
3. Gymnasium
4. Squash Courts
5. CO's Quarters
6. M & E Plinth
7. Pump House
8. Barber's/Shoemaker's/Tailor's Shop
9. Pillboxes
10. Control Tower
11. Night Flying Equipment Store
12. Floodlight Tractor and Trailer Shed
13. Dispersal
14. Battle Headquarters
15. Sleeping Quarters and Kitchen (remains of)
16. Flight Office
17. Latrines
18. Electrical Sub-stations
19. High-level Water Tank
20. Pump House
21. Transit Shed
22. Main Stores
23. Flight Office

(Reproduced from 1996 Landranger 144
1:50000 map by permission of Ordnance Survey
on behalf of the Controller of Her Majesty's
Stationery Office, Crown Copyright Licence
MC99/281)

The flying surfaces at Bodney are now totally unrecognisable, as witnessed by this view through the control tower window.

This picket post guarded the main domestic site on the north side of Bodney.

Now part of STANTA, the high-level water tank and pump house still serve Bodney Camp.

Unsung but essential, these former latrine blocks survive on the eastern side of the airfield.

This imposing pillbox was part of the battle headquarters complex - nearby, a now-sealed underground bunker would have directed airfield defence operations in the event of a ground attack.

Below: Bodney's main stores are in agricultural use and survive in excellent condition.

Deopham Green

One of mid-Norfolk's bleaker corners, the former airfield of Deopham Green has a windswept and particularly eerie atmosphere. It was constructed in 1943 as USAAF Station 142, and was one of a mere handful of Norfolk airfields to host the legendary B17 Flying Fortress. Boeing's 'Queen of the Skies' became the symbol of the 8th AF's daylight bombing campaign, eclipsing the less glamorous but more numerous B24 Liberator much as the Spitfire eclipsed the Hurricane in RAF service.

The 452nd Bomb Group commenced operations on 5th February 1944 (same day as the 453rd BG at Old Buckenham) and, over 250 missions, was to compile a particularly chequered history. The Group had the unenviable record of losing nine commanding officers in 17 months, several of them being lost in action. It also had the dubious distinction of being the first to drop petroleum jelly bombs, known in later wars as napalm. In addition, the 452nd took part in the nerve-rending 'shuttle' missions that involved epic flights across enemy territory to reach airfields in the Soviet Union.

Every 8th AF Bomb Group has its tales of outstanding heroism in the most appalling circumstances, but few compare to the saga of the 452nd B17 'Lady Janet' and the mission to bomb-marshalling yards at Saarbrucken on 9th November 1944. Piloted by 1st Lieutenant Donald J. Gott and 2nd Lieutenant William E. Metzger, 'Lady Janet' was crippled by intense flak which took out three engines and set the aircraft on fire. Gott gave the order to bale out, but the Radio Operator had been severely wounded and was lying unconscious. Gott and Metzger opted to stay with the aircraft and attempt to reach friendly territory, Gott selflessly handing his parachute to a gunner whose own had been damaged beyond use. Unfortunately, during an attempted crash-landing 'Lady Janet' exploded, killing the three on board. Gott and Metzger were posthumously awarded the Medal of Honour.

Even as the War drew to its close the 452nd remained locked in a bitter struggle. The unit received a Distinguished Unit Citation for its attack on the Luftwaffe airfield at Kaltnekirchen on 7th April 1945. A formidable defending force included Me262 jets, and four B17s were lost, two of them being rammed by Fw190s believed to belong to the so-called 'Sturmgruppe' suicide unit. Against this the 452nd claimed 14 enemy aircraft, and their DUC was to be the final one awarded in World War 2.

The 452nd left Deopham in August 1945, after an exhausting campaign during which they lost a total of 160 aircraft. The airfield was turned over to RAF Maintenance Command, finally closing in 1959. Today the site has reverted to agriculture; the runways, however, remain in suprisingly good condition, and one of them has become a public road. For a most evocative drive, take the route between Bush Green and Deopham Stalland, and let your wheels touch the ground from which mighty Fortresses flew.

Deopham Green – Operational History

Unit	Aircraft type	Resident	Role
452nd BG (US 8thAF) 728th, 729th, 730th, 731st Bomb sqns	B17G Flying Fortress	Jan 44–Aug 45	Heavy day bombing

Deopham Green Plan

Quarter-mile approx.

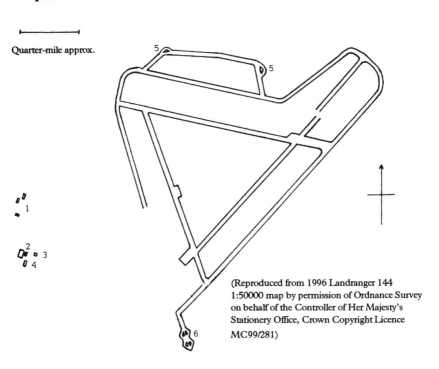

(Reproduced from 1996 Landranger 144 1:50000 map by permission of Ordnance Survey on behalf of the Controller of Her Majesty's Stationery Office, Crown Copyright Licence MC99/281)

Key

1. Domestic Site
2. Gymnasium and Squash Courts
3. Picket Post
4. Mess Hall (Nissen)
5. Loop Dispersals
6. 'Double-Loop' Dispersals

24

Something of Deopham's bleak atmosphere is captured in this view of the former NE-SW runway, part of which is today a public road. Two-wheeled transport occupies the spot where B17s once lifted off, many destined never to return.

The memorial to the 452nd Bomb Group.

This accommodation block is one of several dispersed buildings that survive adjacent to the former airfield.

Docking

Docking is one of Norfolk's most obscure airfield sites. All but invisible on modern maps, it remains reclusive even to the informed visitor. The site was first used in early 1940 as a decoy for Bircham Newton, just 3 miles to the south. Fake Lockheed Hudsons, made from wood and canvas, dotted the field, while at night a dummy flarepath successfully drew German raiders. By the summer Docking was in use as a genuine Relief Landing Ground for Bircham, a role it maintained throughout the war. The deception was not over, however, and in 1941 mock Hawker Hurricanes were deployed in an effort to convince the enemy a major fighter force was active in North Norfolk. Again the spoof was a success, drawing at least one attack.

Despite handling a vast amount of traffic from late 1941 onwards, Docking was never extensively developed, remaining an all-grass field even for heavier aircraft types such as Warwicks, Wellingtons and Whitleys. Wartime photographs show a number of simple blister-type hangars on the southern edge of the field, although no more than routine maintenance was conducted.

Docking's operational career came to an abrupt end in September 1945, and by 1958 the site had been sold off, and quickly reverted to agriculture. Today, most of the surviving buildings are on private land; however, with a little planning it is possible to circumnavigate the airfield and obtain some evocative views across the former flying surface. Leaving Docking village via the Brancaster road will take you along the western edge of the site, and a handful of dispersed buildings can be glimpsed on the left. After about a mile, the road forks by a small wood which contains further buildings now used for agricultural storage. Taking the right fork towards Brancaster Staithe, you will eventually reach a crossroads: turn right, then right again at the next crossroads. After roughly half a mile, the road becomes concrete and you are on the surviving eastern section of perimeter track. At yet another crossroads, turn right to head back towards the village. Along this southern edge the control tower can be seen across the fields, while to your left Bircham Newton looms on the high ground, overlooking its former satellite.

The following list of units operating from Docking needs to be approached with some caution. Consult any three reference books on Norfolk airfields and you will likely get three different lists of squadrons for this location. Confusion arises mainly because units were nominally based at Bircham, but flew from Docking when the parent station was overloaded. To all intents and purposes the aircraft were based at Docking, but returned to Bircham for overhaul. That said, a great deal of published information is incomplete and occasionally contradictory, so that this is best regarded as a list of units seen at Docking, rather than definitely based there. Docking's past seems as obscure and hidden as its surviving monuments, and a definitive history of this busy field has yet to be compiled.

Docking – Operational History

Unit	Aircraft Type	Resident	Role
812 sqn	Swordfish	Spring 40	Mine-laying (day/night)
1403(Met) flt	Blenheim	Spring 40	Weather reconnaissance
235 sqn	Blenheim If	Jul 40–Jun 41	Anti-shipping/convoy patrol
206 sqn	Hudson I	Sep 40	Coastal patrol
1401(Met) flt	Blenheim Hurricane Spitfire, Gladiator	Mar 41–Jul 42	Weather reconnaissance
53 sqn	Blenheim IV	Jul 41–Oct 41	Anti-submarine patrol/ Shipping strike
225 sqn	Lysander III Hurricane I, II Mustang I	Jul 41–Aug 42	Army co-operation/ North Sea reconnaissance/ air-sea rescue
241 sqn	Tomahawk II	Aug. 41	Army co-operation/patrol
22/1522 BAT flt	Oxford I	Oct 41–Apr 42	Blind landing training
288 sqn	Hudson GR III Oxford II, Defiant I Lysander I, II Hurricane I	Jul 41–Aug.42	Target towing
221 sqn	Wellington Ic, VIII	Dec.41–Jan 42	Long-range anti-shipping
268 sqn	Tomahawk IIa	Dec.41–Apr 42	Army co-operation/ patrol
502 sqn	Whitley V, VII	Jan 42–Feb 42	Long-range anti-submarine
235 sqn	Beaufighter Ic	May 42–Jul 42	Strike/convoy protection
143 sqn	Blenheim IVc Beaufighter Ic	Jul 42–Aug 42	Anti-shipping patrol
254 sqn	Beaufighter VIf	Oct.42–Nov 42	Anti-shipping patrol
No.2 APC	Martinet	Nov 42–Feb 45	Target towing
407 sqn	Hudson V Wellington XI	Nov 42–Feb 43	Maritime reconnaissance
53 sqn	Whitley VII	Feb 43–Apr 43	Long-range anti-submarine
415 sqn	Hampden	Feb 43–May 43	Torpedo bombing
304 sqn	Wellington Ic, X	Apr 43–Jun 43	Anti-shipping patrol
1525 BAT flt	Oxford I	Apr 43–Jul 45	Blind landing training
1401(Met) flt	Gladiator II	Apr 43–Sep 43	Weather reconnaissance
Warwick TU	Warwick	Jun 43–Jul 43	Training on Vickers Warwick
519 sqn	Ventura V	Aug 43–Dec 43	Weather reconnaissance

521 sqn	Hampden I Hudson III Ventura V Gladiator II Spitfire IX Mentor Tiger Moth	Sep 43–Nov 44	Weather reconnaissance
415 sqn	Wellington XIII	Nov 43–Jul 44	Anti-shipping patrol (night)
288 sqn	Oxford Martinet	Nov 43–Jul 44	Target towing
855 sqn	Avenger I	May 44–Oct 44	Torpedo bombing
524 sqn	Wellington XIV	May 44–Oct 44	Anti-shipping patrol
288 sqn	Oxford	May 45–Jul 45	Target towing
1693 ASR TU	Wellington III Warwick ASR. I	May 45–Jul 45	Air-sea rescue training

Notes

Weather reconnaissance was a vital but unsung aspect of the air war. 521 sqn was formed out of various Met flts, which is one reason why it acquired such a motley collection of aircraft types. The Hampdens, Hudsons and Venturas conducted long-range weather recon; the Gladiators local recon and the Spitfires high-altitude recon. The Miles Mentors and de Havilland Tiger Moths were retained for communication flights.

Docking at Dusk. This view, looking north from the southern perimeter track, shows how completely the former airfield has returned to agriculture. When operational, two grass runways (nos. 2 & 3) would have been visible from this spot.

Docking Plan

Quarter-mile approx.

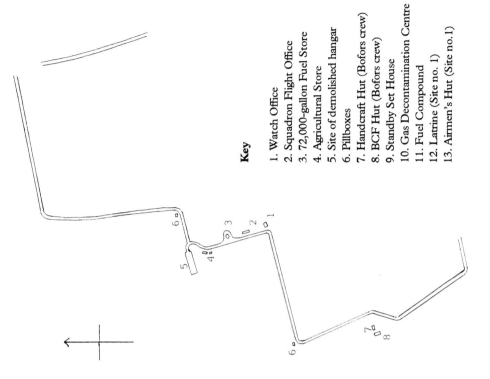

Key

1. Watch Office
2. Squadron Flight Office
3. 72,000-gallon Fuel Store
4. Agricultural Store
5. Site of demolished hangar
6. Pillboxes
7. Handcraft Hut (Bofors crew)
8. BCF Hut (Bofors crew)
9. Standby Set House
10. Gas Decontamination Centre
11. Fuel Compound
12. Latrine (Site no. 1)
13. Airmen's Hut (Site no.1)

(Reproduced from 1996 Landranger 144
1:50000 map by permission of Ordnance Survey
on behalf of the Controller of Her Majesty's
Stationery Office, Crown Copyright Licence
MC99/281)

Battered but unbowed, Docking's Watch Office still stands after sixty years.

The standby set house was part of the communal site. In wartime it would have contained up to three emergency Diesel generators.

This handcraft hut, and the British Concrete Federation hut beyond, housed crews manning the airfield's Bofors defences.

A view of the fuel compound, with the Decontamination Centre in the background

Downham Market

Few ghost fields have suffered as badly in the modern era as Downham Market. It is doubtful whether more than a handful of the motorists travelling the A10 trunk road section between Bexwell and Stow Bardolph have any idea they are crossing a former airfield - the only visual clue for even the informed observer being the large radio masts denoting the eastern and western extremities of the site. In fact the A10 roughly follows the line of the former north-east/south-west runway, and just before the Bexwell roundabout passes a short section of concrete to the east that is the only remaining fragment of the main east-west runway. A third runway, that ran north-west/south-east, has been completely erased.

Downham Market airfield (known as Bexwell among locals) was built slowly in 1941-42, and in 1943 it acquired a feature that made it highly unusual. FIDO (Fog Intensive Dispersal Operation) was a system by which vaporised petrol was burned alongside the main runway; the heat lifted the fog and enabled take-offs and landings to be made in zero-visibility conditions. While FIDO in action was a perfect vision of Hell, it made a significant contribution to poor-weather operations and undoubtedly saved many a weary crew from the trauma of attempting blind landings. Appropriately, the site of the FIDO pumping installation is now occupied by a petrol station.

The airfield has another, more significant claim to fame, in that two from Bomber Command's disproportionately small tally of Victoria Crosses were awarded to Downham airmen, both of them posthumously.

On the night of 12-13th August 1943, Flight-Sergeant Arthur Aaron was flying a 218 sqn Stirling on a raid against Turin. The aircraft was attacked by a German night-fighter, Aaron sustaining horrendous injuries. Despite his wounds, he continued to help the other crew members fly the plane to North Africa, where they landed with great difficulty at Bone airfield, Algeria. Aaron died shortly afterwards, having laboured through unimaginable pain to save his crew and aircraft.

On 4th August 1944, Squadron-Leader Ian Bazalgette of 635 sqn flew a Lancaster on a daylight raid against the V1 flying-bomb storage site at Troissey St Maxim, France. On approach to the target the bomber was hit by anti-aircraft fire, disabling two engines and setting the starboard wing and fuselage aflame. Despite the damage, Bazalgette pressed on to mark the target, then ordered his crew to abandon the aircraft. Most did; however the Bomb Aimer and Mid-Upper Gunner had been severely wounded and could not bail out. Bazalgette attempted to crash-land the Lanc, but as it touched earth it exploded, killing all three. Stories such as these illustrate the appalling risks taken by Bomber Command crews, both by night and by day, over enemy territory.

Downham closed in 1946 and was sold off in 1958. Today, although the flying surfaces have gone, much of the perimeter track survives - indeed the western section is now a public footpath, making this one of the easier Ghost Fields to explore. As with so many former airfields, the Technical Site has been absorbed by a thriving industrial estate, leading to the survival of many buildings. Of particular note is the Guardroom, which is now a showroom for Bexwell Kitchens, while the premises of Bexwell Tractors feature a number of wartime structures.

Aaron and Bazalgette are commemorated by a memorial in front of Bexwell church, but to my mind the surviving remnants of their former base constitute a more tangible - and worthy - monument to their ultimate sacrifice.

Downham Market – Operational History

Unit	Aircraft Type	Resident	Role
218 sqn	Stirling I, III	Jul 42–Mar 44	Heavy night bombing
623 sqn	Stirling III	Aug 43–Dec 43	Heavy night bombing
214 sqn	Stirling I, III	Dec 43–Jan 44	Heavy night bombing
635 sqn	Lancaster I, III, VI	Mar 44–Sep 45	Heavy night bombing (Pathfinder)
571 sqn	Mosquito B.XVI	Apr 44	Fast night strike (Pathfinder)
608 sqn	Mosquito XX, XVI, XXV	Aug 44–Aug 45	Light night strike (Pathfinder)

Notes

635 sqn conducted the operational trials of the Lancaster Mk VI, an unusual variant of this most famous RAF bomber. Fitted with four-bladed propellers and Merlin 28 engines, and stripped of nose and mid-upper gun turrets, the Mk VI was loaded with radar-jamming equipment.

From April 43 to March 44 Downham was used for the storage of Horsa assault gliders destined for use in the D-Day invasion.

Downham Market Plan

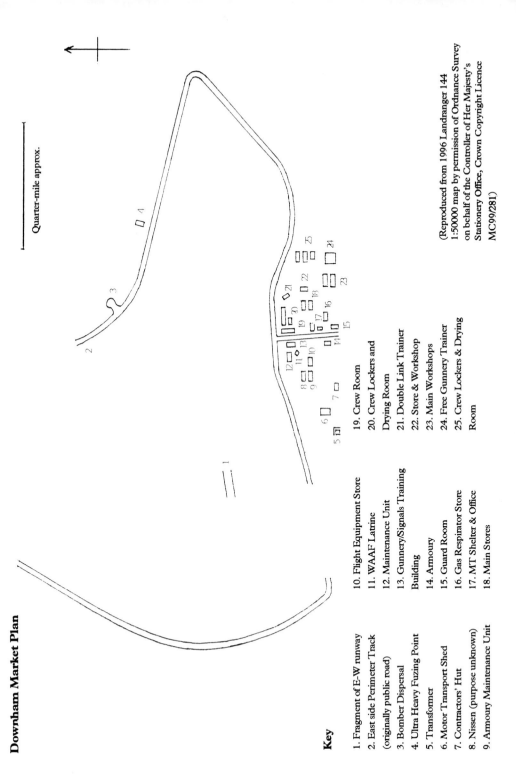

Quarter-mile approx.

Key

1. Fragment of E-W runway
2. East side Perimeter Track (originally public road)
3. Bomber Dispersal
4. Ultra Heavy Fuzing Point
5. Transformer
6. Motor Transport Shed
7. Contractors' Hut
8. Nissen (purpose unknown)
9. Armoury Maintenance Unit
10. Flight Equipment Store
11. WAAF Latrine
12. Maintenance Unit
13. Gunnery/Signals Training Building
14. Armoury
15. Guard Room
16. Gas Respirator Store
17. MT Shelter & Office
18. Main Stores
19. Crew Room
20. Crew Lockers and Drying Room
21. Double Link Trainer
22. Store & Workshop
23. Main Workshops
24. Free Gunnery Trainer
25. Crew Lockers & Drying Room

This small patch of concrete is all that remains of three heavy-bomber runways.

An ultra-heavy fuzing point, on the eastern side of the field, is the only remnant of the former bomb dump.

Downham's flying surfaces may have been all but erased, but much of the technical site remains intact, as shown in this view of the Crew Lockers & Drying Room.

This transformer continues to serve its original function, now as part of Bexwell Industrial Estate. Note the blast wall.

Downham's wartime history is literally etched into some of its surviving buildings.

Dispersed well to the east of the main airfield, this was part of the WAAF accommodation site.

The well-preserved 'frying-pan' dispersal.

The former Guard Room, now a showroom for Bexwell Kitchens.

East Wretham

Constructed between late 1939 and mid-1940 as a satellite to Honington, East Wretham was a very basic all-grass airfield. Wellington bombers, normally based at Honington, were to be seen at the site from spring 1940, but the first permanent residents were 311sqn, comprised of Czech personnel, and their attendant Czech Training Unit (later 1429 Flt).

By late 1942 the field had been re-designated as one of several satellites to Mildenhall, and rare Lancaster IIs supplanted the familiar 'Wimpeys'. This situation persisted until the autumn of 1943, when East Wretham was handed over to the USAAF to become Station 133.

The 359th Fighter Group comprised three squadrons, and like most groups engaged in bomber escort was initially equipped with Republic's mighty P47 Thunderbolt. Steel matting runways were laid in order to accommodate these exceptionally large and heavy fighters. Later the Group re-equipped with various marks of North American P51 Mustang, unquestionably the finest escort fighter of the Second World War.

The 359th received a Distinguished Unit Citation for its action of 11th September 1944, when it claimed 26 enemy fighters. Among the Group's outstanding pilots were Capt. Roy Wetmore, who ended the War with 22½ victories, and Capt. Crenshaw, who on 26th November 1944 attained 'ace' status in one day, with five Fw190s confirmed shot down. By the war's end the 359th had flown 346 missions, and been credited with 263 ærial victories plus 100 more aircraft destroyed on the ground. They had lost a total of 106 of their own aircraft.

From 1946-48 East Wretham was used as a resettlement camp for Polish military personnel who were unable to return to their homeland. Today, the northern part of the site retains its military links as part of the Stanford Training Area. The Army maintains two camps here, and a few wartime structures can still be seen, including a T2 hangar. By contrast, the southern part of the airfield has reverted to heathland and is now a nature reserve. Throughout much of 2001 the site was closed to the public in order to protect the resident 'Flying Flock' of rare sheep from foot and mouth, but happily has reopened and is well worth a visit, not least for a view of the well-preserved remnants of the former bomb dump.

East Wretham Operational History

Unit	Aircraft Type	Resident	Role
311 sqn	Wellington Ia, Ic	Sep 40-Apr 42	Night Bombing
CTU/1429 flt	Wellington Ic Oxford I	Nov 40-Jul 42	Bombing training

115 sqn	Wellington III Lancaster II	Nov 42-Aug 43	Heavy night bombing
LCU/1678HCU	Lancaster II	Mar 43-Aug 43	Bombercrew training
359th FG (US 8thAF 368th, 369th, 370th Fighter Sqns	P47D Thunderbolt P51B, C, D, K Mustang	Oct 43-Nov 45	Bomber escort/ Ground attack

East Wretham Plan

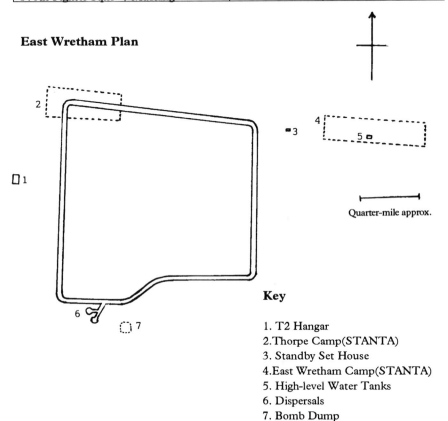

Quarter-mile approx.

Key

1. T2 Hangar
2. Thorpe Camp(STANTA)
3. Standby Set House
4. East Wretham Camp(STANTA)
5. High-level Water Tanks
6. Dispersals
7. Bomb Dump

Now a nature reserve, East Wretham heath betrays very little of its airfield career in this view looking directly north across the site. Note the sheep, part of the 'Flying Flock' that helps to maintain the balance of vegetation.

Part of the well-preserved bomb dump, publicly accessible on the southern side of the heath.

Thorpe Camp, an impressive collection of latter-day Nissen-type huts, occupies the former technical site. It houses troops participating in STANTA exercises.

Fersfield

In 1943, in an especially quiet corner of south Norfolk, construction began of an airfield specifically for American use. Originally known as Winfarthing, it eventually opened in June 1944 as Fersfield. The site was to have a brief yet dramatic operational career, marked by equal parts of tragedy and triumph, securing this gentle backwater a key place in military aviation history.

The so-called 'V' (for Vergeltungswaffe, or Revenge) weapons, with which Nazi Germany attempted to stem the turning tide of war in Western Europe, are well known. The V1, or 'Doodlebug', was a pilotless flying bomb (the Fieseler 103), and was first deployed in the summer of 1944. What is less well known is that the Americans had been working on a flying-bomb concept of their own, and the appearance of the V1, heralding a potentially devastating new phase of warfare, spurred a rush to operational development against it.

In essence the plan was brutally simple. War-weary bombers, unfit for combat, would be stripped out and packed with high explosive, then guided by radio-control from accompanying 'Mother' aircraft onto difficult targets, especially V1 launch-sites. Both Air Force and US Navy were working on radio-control projects, and personnel of both services comprised the ultra-secret 562nd Bomb Squadron when it took up residence at Fersfield (Station 140). The Air Force project was code-named 'Aphrodite', the Navy's 'Anvil' - names that would achieve equal infamy with their Nazi opposites.

One very serious drawback that immediately presented itself was that the drone aircraft (or 'Babies') would have to be piloted for take-off and initial climb until the Mother established control, at which point the 2-man crew would abandon ship. Given that each Baby would contain up to ten tons of highly unstable Torpex, the crews who agreed to fly them were of a very special breed.

The first Aphrodite mission took place on 4th August 1944. Four Mothers and Babies were launched that day, and things very quickly went wrong. Aboard Baby 8 - an ex-351st BG B17G - the crew of Lt John Fisher and T/Sgt Elmer Most realised that a faulty altimeter was causing the aircraft to climb too fast on autopilot. The situation rapidly became critical, and Most bailed out while Fisher struggled to keep control of the heavily-laden bomber, to no avail. Baby 8 stalled and crashed with an apocalyptic explosion in Watling Wood, Sudbourne Park, Suffolk, leaving a huge crater known to this day as 'Fisher's Lake'. The other three Babies had more success, but the results were not encouraging: one had to be flown into the coastal batteries at Gravelines after the Mother lost control; the second overshot its cloud-obscured target by 700 yards; the third impacted 500 yards short of the target due to imprecise control inputs from the Mother. All in all, it was an inauspicious start.

On 12th August it was the Navy's turn, and tragedy was again to strike the 562nd. Piloting the Baby - a navalised PB4Y Liberator - was Lt Joseph Kennedy, brother of future US President John Kennedy. The target was a V1 site at Mimoyecques, but at 2000 ft over Southwold the aircraft inexplicably exploded with the loss of pilot and engineer. For the Kennedy family it was the first of many tragedies to come. For Anvil it was a major setback.

Missions continued sporadically through September and October, with very limited success (one Baby was confidently flown into the wrong target, another flatly refused to obey its Mother and was lost somewhere over southern Sweden). In November the 562nd decamped to Knettishall in Suffolk, where the whole robot aircraft project would eventually be abandoned.

Fersfield reverted to RAF control, and was used as a training centre for aircrew joining 2 Group units on the Continent. But Fersfield was to be the site of one last, legendary mission - one that in success almost made up for the abject failure of the Americans. In March 1945 Mosquitos of 21, 464 and 487 sqns deployed to the field from bases in Belgium, and on the 20th, escorted by Mustangs of 54 sqn, they carried out one of the most audacious and daring attacks of the entire war - an ultra low-level, daylight precision raid on the Shellhaus building in Copenhagen, HQ of the Gestapo in Denmark. Unsurprisingly, the attack was not 100% successful - one group of aircraft mistakenly attacked a nearby school, while four Mosquitos and two Mustangs failed to return - however the Shellhaus was set ablaze and its crucial files on the Danish Resistance destroyed.

At the end of 1945 Fersfield closed for good. Since then the site has fallen into agricultural and industrial use, but a few key buildings remain, as do a couple of dispersed sites, albeit in poor condition. Quite how this place has not become a shrine in the manner of Seething or Thorpe Abbotts is a mystery, given the extraordinary dramas that unfolded here; perhaps that might yet change.

Fersfield Operational History

Unit	Aircraft Type	Resident	Role
562nd BS (USAAF/ USN)	B17F, G Flying Fortress B24D/PB4Y Liberator B34 Ventura	Jul 44 – Jan 45	Aphrodite/Anvil Project
2 Group SU	Mosquito T.III Boston IIIa Hurricane IV Martinet TT. III Mitchell III, Anson I	Dec 44–Dec 45	Aircrew Training

2 Group Training flt	Mosquito T.III	Apr 45-Dec 45	Aircrew/gunnery training

Fersfield Plan

Quarter-mile approx.

Key

1. T2 Hangar
2. Main Workshops
3. Operations Block

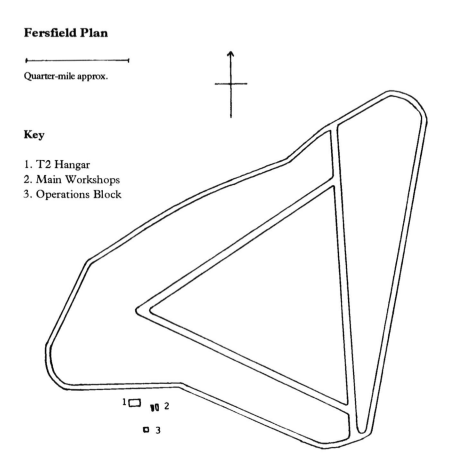

(Reproduced from 1996 Landranger 144 1:50000 map by permission of Ordnance Survey on behalf of the Controller of Her Majesty's Stationery Office, Crown Copyright Licence MC99/281)

Fast disappearing into dense undergrowth are the remains of Fersfield's site no. 12, dispersed about half-a-mile south of the main airfield complex.

The operations block is by far the most significant building to survive at Fersfield. Here detailed planning for 'Anvil' and 'Aphrodite' missions would have been conducted.

42

Foulsham

Constructed in 1941-42, Foulsham airfield was purpose-built with concrete runways and dispersals. Initially under the control of 2 Group, Bomber Command, its early squadrons conducted light bombing operations. Among these was no. 320, formed from a nucleus of Dutch naval personnel who escaped the occupation of Holland in 1940.

On September 1st 1943 the station was transferred to 3 Group, and became home to much heavier metal in the form of Lancaster bombers. Also at this time an unusual unit, the USAAF's 357th Servicing Squadron, moved in to carry out modifications on Mosquitos for the photo-reconnaissance role.

Foulsham's story kicked into high gear when it became one of the many Norfolk airfields assigned to the new 100 Group. Now its squadrons, beginning with no. 192, were tasked with gathering electronic intelligence by monitoring enemy transmissions, and later with developing appropriate countermeasures.

In late 1944 the field was further enhanced by the installation of the FIDO fog-control system, but despite this Foulsham did not remain operational for long after the war, closing to flying in June 1946. Mosquito aircraft destined for scrapping were stored at the site into the late 1940s, and the US Army used part of the airfield until 1955. Today little remains of the runways, and it would be hard to identify the site were it not for the impressive collection of hangars still standing, many of which have been re-clad. These and a handful of other buildings are now part of a rather seedy industrial estate, as has been the fate of so many World War 2 airfields. What does survive is very easily viewed by following the triangle of minor roads between Wood Norton and Foulsham village.

Foulsham Operational History

Unit	Aircraft Type	Resident	Role
98 sqn	Mitchell II	Oct 42- Aug 43	Light bombing (day)
180sqn	Mitchell II	Oct 42- Aug 43	Light bombing (day)
12 GMS	Horsa	Apr 43-Mar 44	Glider storage/maintenance
320 sqn	Mitchell II	Jun 43-Aug 43	Light bombing
1678 HCU	Lancaster II	Sep 43-Dec 43	Bomber conversion
514 sqn	Lancaster II	Sep 43-Nov 43	Heavy night bombing
375th SS (USAAF)	Mosquito F8	Oct 43-Feb 44	Mosquito modification
192 sqn	Halifax II, III, V Mosquito IV, PR.XVI, Anson I Wellington X,	Oct 43-Feb 44	Electronic intelligence/ jamming

1473 flt	Wellington III, Anson I	Dec 43-Feb 44	Electronic intelligence
BSDU	Mosquito FB.VI, NF.XIX	Apr 44-Dec 44	Electronics trials
7th PG (R) (USAAF)	P38J(F5) Lightning	Aug 44-Mar 45	Electronic intelligence
171 sqn	Stirling III Halifax III	Sep 44-Oct 44	Radar Jamming training
462 sqn	Halifax III	Dec 44-Sep 45	Radio countermeasures
199 sqn	Halifax III	Jul 45-Jun 46	Radar test/evaluation

Foulsham Plan

Quarter-mile approx.

Key

1. B1 Hangar
2. T2 Hangars
3. Fire Tender Shed
4. Workshops
5. Fuzing Point

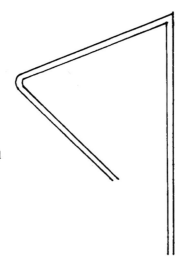

By far the best preserved part of Foulsham is shown here, with the adjacent black T2 hangars framing the former workshops, now painted white for a pleasing contrast.

Apart from hangars, very few buildings remain at Foulsham - this Fire Tender Shed is a noteworthy exception.

Great Massingham

The village of Great Massingham, with its greens, duck-ponds and the legendary Rose and Crown inn, is one of the most picturesque in Norfolk. By contrast, the airfield that shares its name, and that still dominates the high ground to the east, is a bleak, windswept place. It originally opened in July 1940 as a satellite of West Raynham, and was a grass airfield until redevelopment in 1943 gave it three concrete runways; by the summer of 1944 it had assumed the shape that survives today.

Massingham's wartime history was dominated by two twin-engine, light bomber types: the indigenous Bristol Blenheim and the American Douglas Boston (known as the Havoc stateside). The RAF's Blenheim squadrons bore the brunt of low-level, daylight operations in the early part of the war, and suffered high losses against enemy flak and fighters. The Boston was tough, fast and packed a punch, proving an ideal replacement for the increasingly obsolescent Blenheim. One Boston squadron - no. 342 - was a Free French unit, among whose targets were, ironically, a number in occupied France.

An exception to the trend of Massingham aircraft types was a brief stay by 90 sqn, equipped with an early mark of the legendary Boeing Flying Fortress. The RAF's operations with this type were catastrophic failures, thanks in part to marked doctrinal differences between the plane's American designers and its British users. Later, in the hands of the US 8th Air Force, the Fortress would become one of the greatest weapons of World War 2.

Following its redevelopment, Massingham hosted another twin-engine type: the fabulous De Havilland Mosquito. Post-war, an important unit was formed at the field, the Central Fighter Establishment. Intended to test, evaluate and develop tactics for the various aircraft types in Fighter Command, the CFE went on to a long and varied history at West Raynham. Massingham itself closed in 1946 and was sold off in 1958. Today, it clings to its aviation heritage as a private airfield, and is easily accessible as part of the perimeter track is now a public footpath. However, apart from the runways, which remain in good condition, there is little to see: a solitary T2 hangar is the only building still standing. By contrast, some of the dispersed structures associated with the station have fared better: on the western side of the village can be found a water tower and a well-preserved RAF gymnasium.

Great Massingham Operational History

Unit	Aircraft Type	Resident	Role
18 sqn	Blenheim IV	Sep 40-Apr 41	Light bombing (low level)
107 sqn	Blenheim IV	May 41-Aug 41	Light bombing (low level)
90 sqn	Fortress I (B17C)	Jun 41-Jul 41	Day bombing (high altitude)

107 sqn	Boston III, IIIa	Jan 42-Aug 43	Light bombing (low level)
342 sqn	Boston IIIa	Jul 43-Sep 43	Light bombing (low level)
1694 Bomber Defence Training Flt	Martinet TT.1	Apr 44-Jul 45	Target towing
169 sqn	Mosquito FB.VI, NF.XIX	Jun 44-Aug 45	Night intruder/day bombing
1692 Bomber Support Training Unit	Mosquito FB.VI, NF.XIX, T.III Beaufighter Vf, Wellington XVIII, Anson I, Oxford II	Jun 44-Aug 45	Interception radar training
CFE	Mosquito, Spitfire (various marks), Tempest II	Oct 44-Aug 45	Testing & evaluation

Notes: 1692 BSTU was affiliated to 100 Group, Bomber Command, and the interception radars in question were employed on night intruder missions.

Sunset over Massingham (see front cover). View from the west side perimeter, looking towards the village, with the T2 hangar on the right. The radio masts in the distance mark the dispersed Domestic Site, where a handful of buildings still stand.

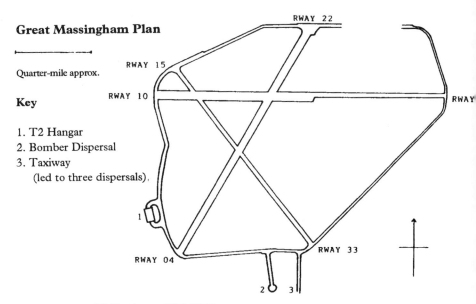

Great Massingham Plan

Quarter-mile approx.

Key

1. T2 Hangar
2. Bomber Dispersal
3. Taxiway
   (led to three dispersals).

RWAY 22
RWAY 15
RWAY 10
RWAY
RWAY 33
RWAY 04

(Reproduced from 1996 Landranger 144 1:50000 map
by permission ofOrdnance Survey on behalf of the Controller of
Her Majesty's Stationery Office, Crown Copyright Licence MC99/281)

A tattered windsock flies over Massingham's southern perimeter track - note the proximity of the church.

Hardwick

REMEMBER THESE MEN BEFORE GOD WITH THANKSGIVING
THE GALLANT CREW OF B24 #42-50597
OF THE 93RD BOMBARDMENT FROM 446TH BG
RAID BE DUSME
WHICH CRASHED IN FOG DURING TAKEOFF
AT HARDWICK, ENGLAND ON 19 DEC 1944
IN A VALIANT ATTEMPT TO DELIVER AIR SUPPORT
TO THE BELEAGUERED GROUND FORCES IN BELGIUM
DURING THE BATTLE OF THE BULGE.
THESE MEN DIED IN THE CAUSE OF FREEDOM.

ROBERT W. MARX, PILOT *   T/SGT BENIAMIN C. WIGA
WILLIAM H. YOUNG, CO-PILOT *   S/SGT FRED D. PETTIGREW
JOHN D. CAMP, NAVIGATOR *   S/SGT RALPH E GIFFORD
DAVID FULLER, JR, BOMBADIER * S/SGT ROBERT A HUGHES
      K. LOCKER   S/SGT HAROLD CLICKMAN
SGT FRANK H. WHITTEN ENGINEER
      BURIED AT THE AMERICAN MILITARY CEMETERY AT CAMBRIDGE
            LEST WE FORGET

This crash-site memorial at Hardwick commemorates just one USAAF crew from the hundreds that lost their lives flying from airfields in the UK.

The airfield at Hardwick was built specifically for the USAAF in 1942, opening in September as Station 104. The site's first occupants were most unusual, being B25C Mitchells of the 310th Bomb Group, part of the 12th Air Force. American-operated B25s were almost unknown in England, and sure enough by November the 310th had moved on to North Africa.

In December came the roar of Liberator bombers, as the 93rd BG moved in from Alconbury (Cambs). The 93rd was already combat-blooded, and during its stay at Hardwick would conduct over 330 missions to run its total to 396 - the highest number carried out by an 8th AF Bomber Group. However, it is important to note that not all these raids were actually launched from Hardwick - the 93rd gained the nickname of 'Travelling Circus' for its many detachments, especially to North Africa. It was during one of these that the 93rd participated in one of the great daylight raids of the War, the attack on the Plœsti oilfields in Romania. The Group received a Distinguished Unit Citation for this mission, one of two awarded for their operations in Africa.

Back in Norfolk, the 93rd joined other Liberator groups in supporting the Allied invasion of occupied Europe. Their targets included such key war-zones as Arnhem and St Lo, and they also helped to ship vital fuel to the armies in France. The final mission was on 25th April 1945, and by July the Group had returned to the States after a gruelling but glorious campaign.

Hardwick passed to the RAF, but never again saw flying units, finally being sold off in 1962. Although the buildings rapidly disappeared, the runways survived, thanks to regular use by crop-dusting aircraft. The field narrowly avoided becoming a landfill site, and survives today in agricultural use, although a gently lifting windsock shows that Hardwick still has life: at the time of writing it housed a very special resident in the form of a beautifully-restored P51 Mustang. In addition, a museum has recently been established on one of the dispersed Accommodation Sites.

Hardwick Operational History

Unit	Aircraft Type	Resident	Role
310th BG (US 12thAF) 379th, 380th, 381st sqns	B25 Mitchell	Sep 42-Nov 42	Medium bombing (tactical)
93rd BG (US 8thAF) 328th, 329th, 330th, 409th Bomb sqns	B24D, E, H, J, L, M Liberator	Dec 42-Jun 45	Heavy day bombing

Hardwick Plan

Quarter-mile approx.

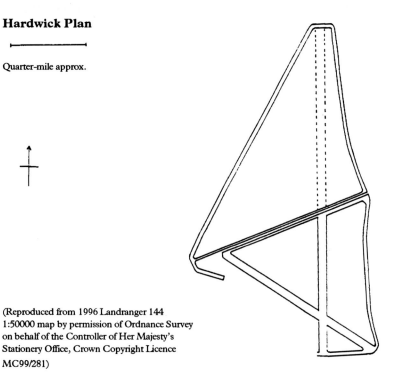

(Reproduced from 1996 Landranger 144
1:50000 map by permission of Ordnance Survey
on behalf of the Controller of Her Majesty's
Stationery Office, Crown Copyright Licence
MC99/281)

50

Down a leafy lane. The approach to Hardwick airfield is today a nondescript track through woodland. Note the modern defences, aimed primarily at the travelling fraternity.

A gently lifting windsock shows that Hardwick still has aviation life. This is the southern edge of the airfield, with the north-east/south-west runway just visible beyond the low earth bank.

Hethel

Hethel was one of the first heavy-bomber bases to be built in Norfolk, construction commencing in 1941 and being completed the following year. It became USAAF Station 114, and its long-term residents were to be the 389th Bomb Group - the 'Sky Scorpions' - who arrived in June 1943. However, like many B24 units nominally based in Norfolk, the 389th was to fly many of its 321 missions while on detachment to North Africa. Among these, very early in the Group's history, was the epic attack on the Ploesti oilfields in Romania. It was for this action that 2nd Lt Lloyd Hughes was posthumously awarded the Medal of Honour, pressing his attack despite his aircraft being terminally damaged on approach to the target. Only two crew members survived the ensuing crash.

The 389th launched its first mission from Hethel on 7th September, but further detachments followed, and it was not until October that the airfield became the Group's permanent home. From then on it was a long, grinding campaign, with mounting losses: seven B24s lost on the Gotha raid of 24th February 1944, and six more attacking Berlin on June 21st. Probably the unkindest cut was 17th April 1945, near the end of the War, when the 389th were inadvertently bombed by a high-level B17 Group attacking French coastal targets - two Liberators being instantly destroyed. The Group suffered a total of 116 losses, but had some consolation in the form of the first-ever Distinguished Unit Citation, awarded for Ploesti.

Unusually for an 8th Air Force station, Hethel was actively used by the RAF in the immediate post-war period. It was finally deactivated in 1948, and sold off in 1964. Ever since, it has maintained a connection with high-performance machines, being the headquarters of Lotus Cars. A modern, high-tech factory has largely swallowed the Technical Site, while parts of the runways are used as a high-speed test track.

Hethel Operational History

Unit	Aircraft Type	Resident	Role
320th BG (US 8thAF)	B26C Marauder	Dec 42-Mar 43	Medium bombing
389th BG (US 8thAF) 564th, 565th, 566th, 567th Bomb sqns	B24D, E, H, J, L, M Liberator	Jun 43-May 45	Heavy day bombing

Note: The 320th BG could only marginally be said to have been 'based' at Hethel. The Group had only a handful of aircraft at this time, and the personnel assigned were almost all ground-crew. As far as is known, no activities apart from the test flights were conducted.

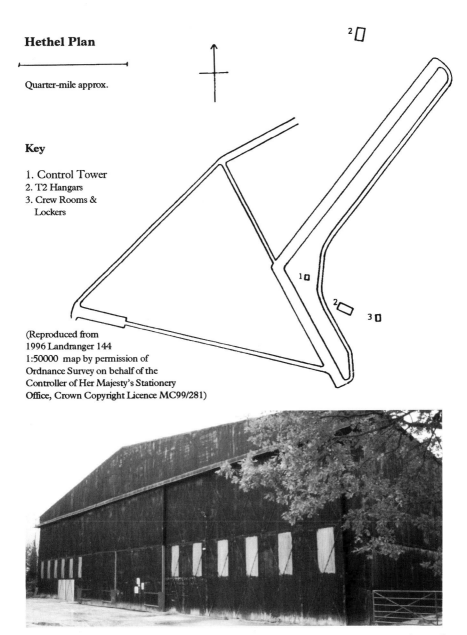

Hethel Plan

Quarter-mile approx.

Key

1. Control Tower
2. T2 Hangars
3. Crew Rooms &
   Lockers

(Reproduced from
1996 Landranger 144
1:50000 map by permission of
Ordnance Survey on behalf of the
Controller of Her Majesty's Stationery
Office, Crown Copyright Licence MC99/281)

The former B24 base at Hethel is famous today for the Lotus car works and test-track occupying the eastern part of the site. However, on the north side can be found this superbly-preserved T2 hangar, now a chemical store.

Langham

Most northerly of all Norfolk's airfields, Langham opened in 1940 as an all-grass satellite to Bircham Newton. First to use the site are believed to have been Royal Navy Swordfish, but in its early months the field was primarily an Emergency Landing Ground for Bircham-based Coastal Command aircraft. Early in 1941 Wellingtons of 300 and 311 sqns, respectively Polish and Czechoslovakian units, used Langham as a forward operating base.

Langham closed in November 1942 for redevelopment: concrete runways were laid, including an extensively lengthened main, running north-east/south-west. Despite this the field continued to be relatively under-used, until the arrival in April 1944 of the most famous unit to operate from Langham, the Beaufighter Strike Wing. Comprised of two squadrons, 455 (Australian) and 489 (New Zealand), the Wing attacked enemy shipping using the Beau's pugnacious combination of nose-mounted cannon and underwing rockets. 455 sqn specialised in taking out flak ships escorting convoys, leaving 489 to attack the larger cargo vessels. During its time at Langham the Wing sank 36 surface vessels and four U-boats.

Previously noted at Docking, 521 sqn brought its considerable meteorological reconnaissance assets to Langham in August '44. In December the unit's flexibility was enhanced by the addition of B17 Fortresses, which provided very long-range weather reports. Other important Coastal operations undertaken from Langham included air-sea rescue and anti-submarine patrols, the latter employing Wellington GR.XIVs equipped with ASV radar and extremely powerful Leigh lights.

Langham remained in use for some time after the War, and in its final incarnation served as an Emergency Landing Ground for the USAF at Sculthorpe, seeing regular detachments by B26 Invader target tugs. Flying finally ceased in November 1958 and the site was sold off in October 1961. Today turkey sheds cover much of the runways, although part of the airfield's southern section is still used by light aircraft. Of the few surviving buildings, easily the best-known is the Dome Trainer, colloquially referred to as the 'Astrodome'. This was used to train anti-aircraft gunners and is one of only a handful still standing. In 1999 it was cosmetically (if somewhat unsympathetically) restored by Bernard Matthews Ltd. Langham is very easily explored, as the minor road between Cockthorpe and Langham village cuts right across the middle of the site. In addition two public footpaths take in parts of the former airfield.

As is the case with Docking, compiling a full list of units operating from Langham is a complex undertaking, the waters being muddied by its function as Bircham's satellite. Units nominally based at Bircham (or even Docking) routinely kept detachments at Langham. The following list, compiled from several published sources, endeavours to be as comprehensive as possible.

Langham - Operational History

Unit	Aircraft type	Resident	Role
1 ACCU (K/M)	Demon, Henley, Defiant TT.III	Dec 41-Nov 42	Target towing
231 sqn (det)	Tomahawk I	1942	Army co-operation
2 sqn (det)	Mustang I	1942	Army co-operation
221 sqn	Wellington GR.VIII	1942	Anti-shipping patrol
206 sqn (det)	Hudson	1942	Coastal patrol
Station flt	Tiger Moth	1942	Communications
819 sqn (RN)	Swordfish I	Jul 42-Aug 42	Night shipping patrol
143 sqn (det)	Blenheim If Beaufighter Ic	Jul 42-Sep 42	Anti-shipping strike
280 sqn	Anson I	Jul 42-Nov 42	Air-sea rescue
254 sqn	Beaufighter 6c	Oct 42-Nov 42	Torpedo strike
1611 TT flt	Henley	Nov 42	Target towing
1612 TT flt	Henley	Nov 42	Target towing
1626 TT flt	Lysander, Henley TT.III Defiant TT.III	Jul 43-Nov 43	Target towing
No.2 AAPC	Martinet	1944	Gunnery practice
455 sqn	Beaufighter TF.X	Apr 44-Oct 44	Anti-shipping strike
489 sqn	Beaufighter TF.X	Apr 44-Oct 44	Anti-shipping strike
524 sqn	Wellington GR.XIII GR.XIV	Jul 44-Oct 44	Anti-submarine patrol
521 sqn	Ventura V, Hudson III, V Spitfire IX GladiatorII Hurricane IIc Fortress II, III (B17F/g)	Aug 44-Dec 45	Weather reconnaissance
280 sqn	Warwick ASR.I	Aug 44-Oct 44	Air-sea rescue
612 sqn	Wellington GR.XIV	Oct 44-Jul 45	Anti-submarine patrol
144 sqn	Beaufighter TF.X	Oct 44-Apr 45	Anti-shipping strike
827 sqn (RN)	Barracuda II	Nov 44-Dec 44	Anti-shipping strike
456 sqn	Mosquito NF30	Mar 45-Jun 45	Night interception
407 sqn	Wellington GR.XIV	Apr 45-May 45	Anti-submarine patrol
279 sqn	Lancaster ASR.3	Sep 45-Mar 46	Air-sea rescue
280 sqn	Warwick I	Nov 45-Jan 46	Air-sea rescue

254 sqn	Beaufighter TF.X	Nov 45-May 46	Coastal strike
1402 (Met) flt	Hurricane Iic	Dec 45-May 46	Weather recon-naissance (local)
1561 (Met) flt	Spitfire	1946	Weather recon-naissance (local)
1562 (Met) flt	Spitfire	1946	Weather recon-naissance (local)
RNLAF Tech Training School	(various static types)	Jul 46-Sep 47	Ground-crew training (Dutch)
2 CAACU	Spitfire LF.XIVe Beaufighter TT.10 Mosquito TT.35 Vampire FB.V, FB.9, T11	Apr 53-Nov 58	Target towing
Marshall's School of Army co-op	Mosquito TT.35	Apr 53-Nov 58	Target tug training

Langham Plan

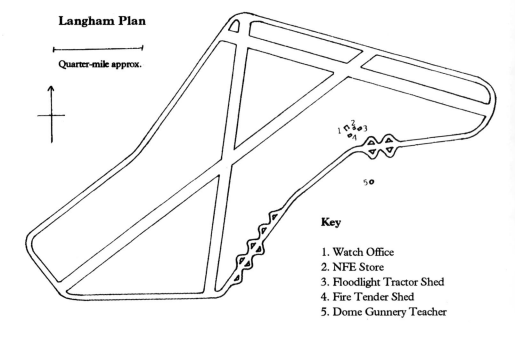

Quarter-mile approx.

Key

1. Watch Office
2. NFE Store
3. Floodlight Tractor Shed
4. Fire Tender Shed
5. Dome Gunnery Teacher

(Reproduced from 1996 Landranger 144 1:50000 map by permission of Ordnance Survey on behalf of the Controller of Her Majesty's Stationery Office, Crown Copyright Licence MC99/281)

A good impression of Langham's extended north-east/south-west runway is given in this view, looking south-west. Note the 'dip' typical of major runways, even at modern military airfields.

Langham's most famous surviving building, the Dome Trainer, was cosmetically restored in 1999.

Still keeping watch: Langham's Watch Office and Fire Tender Shed survive in very good condition. Part of a 'loop' dispersal is visible behind the trees.

Under a brooding sky, a view south along the north-south runway.

Little Snoring

Hands-down winner in the most-delightfully-named airfield category, Little Snoring opened in 1943 as a satellite to Foulsham. In its early months it was assigned to No. 3 Group Bomber Command, and hosted Lancaster IIs which were a very rare sight at the time. With Bristol Hercules engines instead of the more familiar Rolls-Royce Merlins, the MkII was never produced in great quantity.

Towards the end of the year Snoring's career took a very different course as it was transferred to 100 Group, becoming home to a number of squadrons operating the legendary Mosquito. Night Intruder missions were the primary tasking: the 'Mossies' would escort RAF bomber streams over enemy territory, picking off German night-fighters with the assistance of a top-secret homing radar known as 'Serrate'. Later a more advanced radar, the Anti-Surfacer Homer (ASH), enabled the Intruders to freelance and attack the enemy at its home bases. However, Snoring itself was also subject to Intruder attacks - one such on the night of April 19th/20th 1944 put the airfield temporarily out of commission.

Snoring's military use after the war was very brief, and mainly concerned the storage of surplus Mosquitos. Happily, the field passed into civilian hands and continues to be active today, although only part of the site is used for aviation and very few buildings remain. Under the auspices of the McAully Flying Group, Snoring has had a colourful recent history, being the venue for ærobatics competitions and air displays, and it still hosts occasional fly-ins. The field is easily viewed from the minor road between Little Snoring village and Thursford, which actually follows a significant portion of the perimeter track. A number of dispersed buildings survive in and around the village itself.

Little Snoring Operational History

Unit	Aircraft Type	Resident	Role
115 sqn	Lancaster II	Aug 43-Nov 43	Heavy night bombing
1678 HCU	Lancaster II	Aug 43-Sep 43	Bomber crew training
169 sqn	Beaufighter VI Mosquito II	Dec 43-Jun 44	Night Intruder missions
1692 Flt	Defiant I Beaufighter II Anson I, Oxford II Mosquito FB.VI	Dec 43-Jun 44	Radar training

515 sqn	Blenheim V Beaufighter IIf Mosquito II, FB.VI	Dec.43-Jun.45	Night Intruder missions
USAAF Intruder Det	P51 Mustang P38 Lightning	Mar.44-Apr.44	Long-range escort trials
23 sqn	Mosquito FB.VI, NF.30	Jun.44-Sep.45	Night Intruder missions
141 sqn	Mosquito NF.30	Jul.45-Sep.45	Night fighter
No.2 CAACU (Civilian)	Spitfire XVI Mosquito TT.35 Vampire FB.V	Jun.50–Apr 53	Anti-aircraft cooperation

Little Snoring Plan

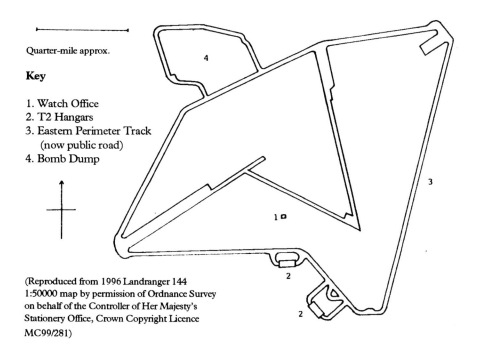

Quarter-mile approx.

Key

1. Watch Office
2. T2 Hangars
3. Eastern Perimeter Track
   (now public road)
4. Bomb Dump

(Reproduced from 1996 Landranger 144 1:50000 map by permission of Ordnance Survey on behalf of the Controller of Her Majesty's Stationery Office, Crown Copyright Licence MC99/281)

59

On a perfectly still midsummer's day, the former Watch Office at Little Snoring lies stranded in a sea of ripening corn. Despite the windsock, the building is totally disused.

The impressive frontage of a T2 hangar, one of two remaining at Snoring.

The road to Thursford follows the airfield's perimeter track, a portion of which is visible in this view, looking east.

Ludham

By far the most easterly of Norfolk's World War 2 airfields, Ludham lies right in the heart of the beautiful and dreamy Broadland district, an area more familiar with boats than aircraft. It was built in 1941 as a satellite to Coltishall, which meant Fighter Command and, inevitably, Spitfires. Continuously developed throughout the war, the 'Spit' was to dominate the early and late history of Ludham, and there would be a vast difference in performance between the Merlin-powered Mk V and the Griffon-engined Mk XVI and 21.

The early Spitfire squadrons at Ludham boasted significant histories: 19 sqn had been responsible for bringing the type into operational service at Duxford, while 610 - one of the most celebrated Auxiliary Squadrons - listed among its pilots 'Johnnie' Johnson, who went on to become the highest-scoring RAF pilot of the war with 38 victories, and whose recent death robbed a nation of one of its greatest war heroes.

The pattern of activity at the field came to an abrupt halt in September 1943. The plan was to develop the site for the USAAF, but this never happened, and for almost a year Ludham was effectively moribund. However, Coltishall units continued to use it for gunnery practice, and its location near the coast made it a haven for shot-up aircraft returning from missions over Occupied Europe.

When the field re-opened in August 1944, it had a different name and a very different role. Now HMS *Flycatcher*, it became HQ for the Royal Navy's Mobile Aircraft Repair and Servicing Organisation. Here servicing units were formed for deployment overseas, and although *Flycatcher* had no aircraft of its own, RN transports were a fairly regular sight.

In February 1945 the RAF, and Spitfires, returned with a vengeance. 603 sqn undertook a variety of operations, which included dive-bombing attacks on V2 rocket sites in Holland. However, by the time 91 sqn arrived with state-of-the-art Mk 21s, the war in Europe was all but over. By August, Ludham's operational career was finished.

Perhaps because of its out-of-the-way location, Ludham has fared rather well in the post-war era. The southern section of the airfield has for many years been used by crop-dusting aircraft, and a significant number of buildings still remain. Of these, by far the most evocative is the Watch Office, and at the time of writing efforts were being made by a group of enthusiasts to have this restored for posterity. Let us hope these efforts are successful.

Ludham Operational History

Unit	Aircraft Type	Resident	Role
19 sqn	Spitfire Vb	Dec 41-Apr 42	Fighter
610 sqn	Spitfire Vb, Vc	Apr 42-Oct 42	Fighter/escort
167 sqn	Spitfire Vb, Vc	Oct 42-May 43	Fighter/ground attack
245 sqn	Typhoon Ib	Mar 43-May 43	Fighter
195 sqn	Typhoon Ib	May 43-Jul 43	Fighter/escort
611 sqn	Spitfire Vb	Jul 43-Aug 43	Fighter/strike
603 sqn	Spitfire XVIe	Feb 45-Apr 45	Fighter/escort/strike
602 sqn	Spitfire XVIe	Feb 45-Apr 45	Fighter/strike
91 sqn	Spitfire 21	Apr 45-Jul 45	Fighter
1 sqn	Spitfire 21	May 45-Jul 45	Fighter

Ludham Plan

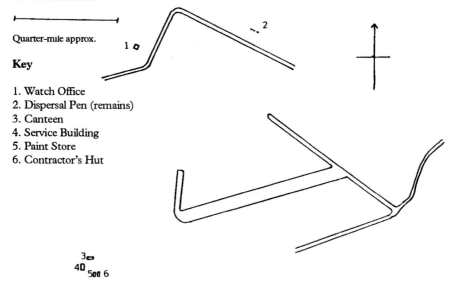

Quarter-mile approx.

Key

1. Watch Office
2. Dispersal Pen (remains)
3. Canteen
4. Service Building
5. Paint Store
6. Contractor's Hut

Part of Ludham remains an active airfield. The attractive Blister Hangar is a post-war addition.

The former Fighter airfield at Ludham still has a purposeful feel about it. This view is looking directly north across the site, with the Watch Office visible in the distance.

This impressive pillbox guards the southern approach to Ludham.

Matlask(e)

A place so obscure that even its spelling is in doubt, Matlask (the 'e' is apparently optional) is a particularly bleak corner of North Norfolk. The airfield was prepared in the crucial summer of 1940 as a satellite to the key Fighter Command station at Coltishall, and came into use in October after attacks on the parent site. Throughout its early years the field was plagued by drainage problems, particularly in the wet wartime winters.

If Matlask has a claim to fame then it rests with the more unusual fighter types that flew from its grass runways. First was the Bell P39 Airacobra, an American design that employed many radical innovations, in particular a centrally-mounted engine and a tricycle undercarriage. Trialled by 601 sqn at Matlask and later Duxford, the P39 was rejected by the RAF but went on to serve the USAAF and Soviet Army Air Force with some distinction.

Next came a British design, the twin-engined Westland Whirlwind. Potentially a world-beater, the Whirlwind was fatally undermined by the unreliability of its Rolls-Royce Peregrine engines. Its reputation was not helped by the infamous participation in operations during the 'Channel Dash' on 12th February 1942. Three German warships - the *Gneisenau, Prinz Eugen* and *Scharnhorst* plus escort - slipped audaciously through the English Channel, defying a host of RAF and FAA attacks against them. 137 sqn launched six Whirlwinds from Matlask, but only two returned from an epic dogfight with covering Bf109s. Later the Whirlwind would tangle with German E-boats, but the type was destined never to be produced in quantity and it fell into obscurity.

Matlask closed in 1943 for development, and was offered to the USAAF which declined to take on the field. Fighters returned with a vengeance in 1944, as a dizzying variety of squadrons - now part of the huge 2nd Tactical Air Force - operated classic types such as Mustangs, Spitfires and Tempests from this small airfield. The hectic pace continued until the end of the war, when suddenly the site fell silent, and by October 1945 the RAF had abandoned it for good. Brief use as a POW camp followed, before agriculture began the inexorable destruction of the field. Today there is virtually nothing save for traces of the perimeter track, and a certain sigh in the wind that speaks of a great history, if you take the time to listen.

Matlask - Operational History

Unit	Aircraft Type	Resident	Role
72 sqn	Spitfire I	Oct 40-Nov 40	Fighter
222 sqn	Spitfire II, Vb	May 41-Jul 41	Fighter/fishery protection

601 sqn	Hurricane II, Airacobra I	Jul 41-Aug 41	Fighter/trials
19 sqn	Spitfire	Aug 41-Dec 41	Fighter
5ASR Flt/278 sqn	Walrus, Lysander I	Oct 41-Aug 42	Air-sea rescue
137 sqn	Whirlwind	Dec 41-Aug 42	Fighter/coastal patrol
56 sqn	Typhoon I	Aug 42-Jul 43	Fighter
56th FG (Det) (US 8th AF)	P47C Thunderbolt	Mar 43-May 43	Firing practise only
1489 Flt	Lysander TT.III, Master, Henley, Martinet	Apr 43-Jun 43	Target towing
611 sqn	Spitfire IX	Jul 43	Fighter
195 sqn	Typhoon Ib	Jul 43-Aug 43	Fighter/strike
609 sqn (Det)	Typhoon Ia, Ib	Jul 43-Aug 43	Fighter/strike
266 sqn (Det)	Typhoon Ib	Aug 43	Fighter/strike
3 sqn	Tempest V	Sep 44	Fighter/strike
56 sqn	Tempest V	Sep 44	Fighter/strike
486 sqn	Tempest V	Sep 44	Fighter/strike
19 sqn	Mustang III	Sep 44-Oct 44	Fighter/strike
65 sqn	Mustang III	Sep 44-Oct 44	Fighter/strike
122 sqn	Mustang III	Sep 44-Oct 44	Fighter/strike
229 sqn	Mustang III	Oct 44-Nov 44	Fighter
453 sqn	Spitfire IX, XVI	Oct 44-Nov 44	Fighter
602 sqn	Spitfire IX,	Oct 44-Nov 44	Fighter
451 sqn	Spitfire XVI	Feb 45-Apr 45	Fighter

A line of trees on the horizon gives a rough visual clue to the direction of one of Matlask's grass runways in this view, looking north-east. Sadly, this is all that can now be discerned of a once-busy Fighter Command station.

Remains of the perimeter track on the east side of the site.

Matlask Plan

Quarter-mile approx.

ɑ 4

2

Key

1. Remains of Technical Site
2. Section of East Perimeter Track
3. Access Road/South Perimeter Track
4. Pillbox

3

(Reproduced from 1996 Landranger 144 1:50000 map by permission of Ordnance Survey on behalf of the Controller of Her Majesty's Stationery Office, Crown Copyright Licence MC99/281)

66

Methwold

Methwold was constructed in 1939 as a satellite for the important bomber base at Feltwell, and like its parent station was originally all-grass. Thus the aircraft type most associated with Feltwell - the Vickers Wellington - was a ubiquitous sight at Methwold in the early years of the war. In fact, between 1940 and 1942 Methwold had no based units of its own, but Feltwell's Wellingtons routinely dispersed there to reduce the threat of attack.

An aircraft type that was to have a particular association with Methwold arrived at the airfield in October 1942: the Lockheed Ventura. This American twin-engined medium bomber was designed to a British specification, but it was not a great success and rapidly earned the nickname of 'The Pig' from its disenchanted crews.

Two Ventura squadrons, 464 and 487, were so-called 'Dominion' squadrons, comprising Australian and New Zealander personnel. One of those New Zealanders, Squadron Leader Leonard Trent of 487, was to be the key figure in the most famous operation conducted from Methwold - an operation that, ironically, signalled the demise of the Ventura in RAF service.

The date was May 3rd, 1943: the mission a 'Circus' or diversionary attack, on the Amsterdam power station. The plan called for strong fighter escort, but this penetrated enemy airspace too early and alerted the Luftwaffe defences. Twelve Venturas took off from Methwold, one returning early with engine trouble. The remainder flew straight into the defending fighter force and were massacred. Only Trent's aircraft made it through to hit the target, after which he too was hit and the bomber went out of control. Trent ordered his crew to bale out, but minutes later the plane exploded, with only Trent and his navigator surviving to become prisoners of war. Trent went on to participate in the legendary 'Great Escape' from Stalag Luft III, and on his return to England in 1945 he received a much-deserved Victoria Cross. The Ventura, incidentally, went on to serve the US Navy with distinction.

In 1943 Methwold was closed to flying as work commenced to build concrete runways and upgrade the field to heavy-bomber status, this being completed in the spring of 1944. In this form Methwold soldiered on until 1946, when it was placed on Care & Maintenance. Unlike many Norfolk airfields, Methwold lingered after the war, and continued to see regular flying: training aircraft from Feltwell used the site, as did aircraft from the Watton-based Central Signals Establishment. The airfield was also very busy with transport aircraft during exercises at the nearby Stanford Battle Training Area. However, it could not last, and the base finally closed in 1958.

Today, Methwold has reverted to agriculture and housing developments have begun to encroach on the site. Despite this, a goodly number of buildings survive and the overall 'feel' of an airfield still persists. Unusually for a ghost field, Methwold is highly accessible; a semi-public road off the B1112 follows the east side perimeter track, and will take you past both the surviving T2 hangars, even as far as the famous gymnasium dispersed to the south of the site.

Although it has totally returned to agriculture, Methwold is still very much an airfield if viewed from the right angle. This is the eastern part of the site, with the perimeter track in the foreground and a very well-preserved T2 hangar on the horizon. The factory just visible in the distance is built on the former site of two further hangars.

Methwold - Operational History

Unit	Aircraft Type	Resident	Role
214 sqn	Wellington I, Ia	Sep 39-Feb 40	Shipping patrol
57 sqn	Wellington Ic, III	Jan 42-Sep 42	Heavy night bombing
21 sqn	Ventura I, II	Oct 42-Apr 43	Light bombing
320 sqn	Mitchell II	Mar 43	Medium bombing
464 sqn	Ventura I, II	Apr 43-Jul 43	Light bombing
487 sqn	Ventura I, II	Apr 43-Jul 43	Light bombing
149 sqn	Stirling III Lancaster I, III	May 44-Apr 46	Heavy bombing
218 sqn	Lancaster I, III	Aug 44-Dec 44	Heavy bombing
207 sqn	Lancaster I, III	Oct 45-Apr 46	Heavy bombing

Notes: 149 sqn undertook a number of interesting missions in addition to their normal heavy bombing operations. In the summer of 1944 they dropped weapon supplies to the French Resistance, and in the spring of 1945 participated in Operation Manna, the air-dropping of food and supplies to the starving Dutch populace.

Horsa assault gliders were stored at Methwold from March '43 to April '44.

Methwold Plan

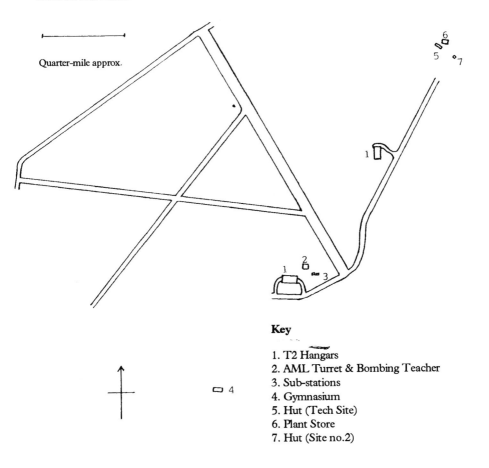

Quarter-mile approx.

Key

1. T2 Hangars
2. AML Turret & Bombing Teacher
3. Sub-stations
4. Gymnasium
5. Hut (Tech Site)
6. Plant Store
7. Hut (Site no.2)

Right: This view along the former north-east/south-west runway clearly shows the reduction to tractor width typical of airfields that have reverted to agricultural use.

Below left: Methwold's best-known building is the former gymnasium, with its cinema extension facing the camera – this would have housed the projection equipment.

Below right: Interior of the gymnasium, now used for agricultural storage. On the far wall can be seen the square projection slots for cinema use. Gyms were among the most versatile buildings on airfields, being also used as chapels, theatres and lecture halls.

North Creake

Set deep in the wilds of North Norfolk, North Creake doesn't advertise itself. However, a run along the B1105 road between Fakenham and Wells-next-the-Sea will offer not only some delightful scenery, but also the opportunity for a spot of time-travel. For this road goes straight through the heart of what is obviously a World War 2 airfield technical site, still bustling with activity. Glancing to the west, one half expects to see heavy bombers running up on the perimeter track. It is an illusion, of course, but North Creake is one of those special ghost fields that has retained its atmosphere along with many of its buildings.

Like so many airfields, North Creake is geographically misnamed, being in fact constructed virtually on top of the deserted mediæval village site of Egmere: this is the name by which it was always known locally. RAF activity at the site began in 1940 with the establishment of a decoy field for Docking (which itself was originally a decoy for Bircham Newton). The decoy operated until 1942, by which time the decision had been taken to develop a full-scale bomber airfield. By 1943 the site was ready, but various operational changes meant that it did not see any flying units until May 1944. And when it did, its out-of-the-way location was put to good use.

Creake was one of several Norfolk airfields assigned to 100 Group, Bomber Command. This secret Group was engaged in developing what would today be termed 'Electronic Warfare', and Creake's squadrons, 199 and 171, primarily undertook the jamming of German radar installations during raids by other Groups. Their main weapon was the famous 'Window' - strips of aluminium foil that generated multiple radar contacts when released at altitude. The success of Bomber Command's night operations depended to a great extent on 100 Group's activities.

After a short operational life, Creake ceased flying in 1945, and after a period of use for storage of surplus Mosquito aircraft, closed in 1947. Today, much of the technical site survives as a thriving light industrial estate, and two of the three T2 hangars, much modified, form part of Dalgety Agriculture's feed mill operation. To the north-east, the dispersed accommodation site survives in agricultural use.

North Creake Operational History

Unit	Aircraft Type	Resident	Role
199 sqn	Stirling III Halifax III	May 44-Jul 45	Radio counter-measures/ night bombing
171 sqn	Stirling III Halifax III	Oct 44-Jul 45	Radio counter-measures/ night bombing

North Creake Plan

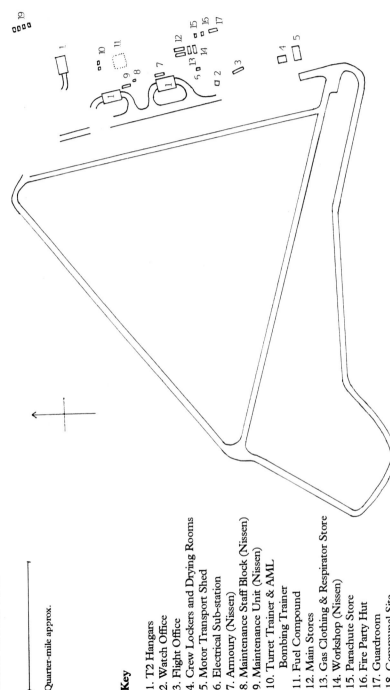

Quarter-mile approx.

Key

1. T2 Hangars
2. Watch Office
3. Flight Office
4. Crew Lockers and Drying Rooms
5. Motor Transport Shed
6. Electrical Sub-station
7. Armoury (Nissen)
8. Maintenance Staff Block (Nissen)
9. Maintenance Unit (Nissen)
10. Turret Trainer & AML
 Bombing Trainer
11. Fuel Compound
12. Main Stores
13. Gas Clothing & Respirator Store
14. Workshop (Nissen)
15. Parachute Store
16. Fire Party Hut
17. Guardroom
18. Communal Site
19. Airmen's Huts (Mess Site)

The former communal site at North Creake is typical of the large number of well-preserved buildings at this site.

Formerly the maintenance unit, this Nissen hut is now part of the Dalgety site. One of the surviving T2 hangars is visible in the background.

Now buried in dense woods, an AML Bombing Teacher.

North Creake's Watch Office has been converted into this attractive private dwelling.

North Pickenham

The modern age has not been kind to North Pickenham airfield - virtually all of its buildings have been erased, and the runways are largely obliterated by turkey sheds. It is almost as if the site were ashamed of its past, and there is a pervading atmosphere of sadness and dereliction. In many ways this is appropriate, for it was from North Pickenham that the most unfortunate of US Eighth Air Force bomber groups conducted its short and disastrous campaign.

Pickenham was the 77th and final British air base to be handed over to the USAAF during World War 2. This took place with a formal ceremony on 27th May 1944, but by this time the last Bomb Group to reach England - the 492nd - was already in residence, and already suffering heavy losses.

On 18th May the Group took part in a raid on Brunswick: heavy fighter attacks saw four aircraft lost before the target; a fifth exploded on its bombing run and three more went down on the return trip.

On 28th June the 8th AF put up over 1400 bombers to attack oil refineries throughout Germany, with the 492nd forming part of the assault on sites at Pollitz and Osterburg. Problems with coordinating so many bombers and their required fighter escort left the Group badly exposed, and Luftwaffe fighters downed fourteen aircraft. The only Liberator to return to North Pickenham was one that had aborted the mission due to engine trouble.

The final straw came on 7th July, with a mission to Merseburg. Again, there were problems coordinating the attacking forces and the 492nd suffered twelve losses to enemy fighters. In August the Group conducted four missions, losing four more planes, but the writing was on the wall. After losing 57 aircraft in just 64 operations, the 492nd was effectively disbanded: its surviving crews were scattered throughout other Bomb Groups, and its designation switched to a Special Operations unit.

In place of the 492nd, to Pickenham from Metfield in Suffolk came the 491st BG - the 'Ringmasters'. As a Group with a superb operational record - just ten losses in three months - the 491st was the ideal antidote to the previous unfortunate residents. The 491st went on to conduct 187 missions up to the end of the war in Europe, with great success. However, on one day - 26th November 1944 - they experienced the kind of attrition that had destroyed their predecessors. Out of the 27 aircraft put up by the Group, 15 were lost on approach to the target. Showing astounding discipline, the tattered remnants formed up and pressed the attack, an action which saw the Group awarded a much-deserved Distinguished Unit Citation.

Post-war, North Pickenham bounced from Bomber Command to the USAF and back again, though it never again hosted operational flying units. In 1958 its surface was scarred by launch-pads for the Thor missiles of 220 sqn. Part of the UK's Cold War deterrent, the Thor was a frankly useless weapon; its only real achievement was to ensure that East Anglia would be a first-strike target in an all-out nuclear war. By 1963 the Thor was obsolete, and Pickenham closed in October of that year. A brief revival came in 1965, when experimental Kestrel VTOL aircraft were flown from the field.

Today, very little remains, although evocative views of the field can be obtained from the B1077, which runs along the southern edge. In the 1980s an ill-fated effort to develop part of the site as an industrial park came to nought, leaving the skeleton of an unfinished warehouse and access roads that go nowhere, further adding to the desolation of this lonely place.

North Pickenham - Operational History

Unit	Aircraft Type	Resident	Role
492nd BG (US 8thAF) 856th, 857th, 858th, 859th Bomb sqns	B24 H, J Liberator	Apr 44-Aug 44	Heavy day bombing
491st BG (US 8thAF) 852nd, 853rd, 854th, 855th Bomb sqns	B24 H, J, L, M Liberator	Aug 44-Jul 45	Heavy day bombing
220 sqn	Thor IRBM	Jul 59-Jul 63	Cold War deterrent

Storm clouds gather over North Pickenham airfield in this view looking north. The row of Ordnance huts on the right mark the location of the former Bomb Dump, while the line of chicken sheds on the horizon follows the north-west/south-east runway. Note the radio mast, a prominent local landmark.

North Pickenham Plan

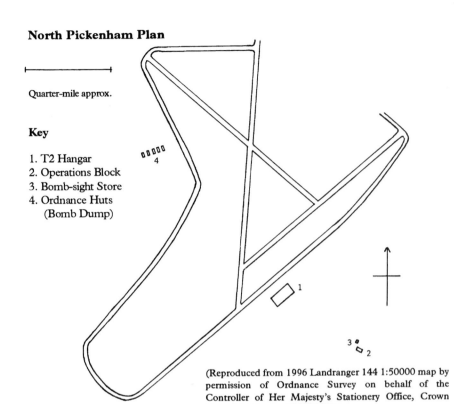

Quarter-mile approx.

Key

1. T2 Hangar
2. Operations Block
3. Bomb-sight Store
4. Ordnance Huts
   (Bomb Dump)

(Reproduced from 1996 Landranger 144 1:50000 map by permission of Ordnance Survey on behalf of the Controller of Her Majesty's Stationery Office, Crown Copyright Licence MC99/281)

The simple but effective memorial in North Pickenham village.

A view of the north-south runway looking due south.

This nondescript-looking building was used to store one of the most significant American weapons of World War 2 - the Norden M7 bombsight.

Old Buckenham

Constructed from 1942-43 specifically as a USAAF heavy-bomber base, Old Buckenham opened in late 1943 as Station 144. Only one Bomb Group, the Liberator-equipped 453rd, was destined to operate from the site, but this unit was one that compiled an unmatched record of success.

Commencing on 5th February 1944, the 453rd carried out 255 missions, and through a potent combination of flying skill and sheer luck, turned in the lowest loss rate of any 8th AF bomber group. Indeed, one squadron - the 733rd - turned in an astonishing record of 82 consecutive operations without losing a single aircraft. Compared to the hellish attrition suffered by other units of the 'Mighty Eighth', the 453rd was a phenomenon. Its one major black spot occurred on 8th April 1944, when seven B24s were lost in a raid on Brunswick.

If the presence of the 453rd wasn't cause enough for Old Buckenham to achieve particular fame, then its Hollywood connections certainly secure a place in popular folklore. The legendary James Stewart served as Group Executive Officer at the field in 1944, while another rather different screen actor was also present, a man who would be known to film-goers as Walter Matthau.

In the summer of 1944 the 453rd took a welcome break from pounding Nazi Germany to drop food supplies to the starving French populace. They eventually left Norfolk in May-June 1945, having conducted, if there is such a thing, an exemplary war. Old Buckenham saw occasional post-war use as a satellite for various RAF maintenance units, and lingered under Air Ministry control until 1960. Today the site has reverted to agriculture, save for a section of the east-west runway which is retained as a light aircraft strip, occasionally hosting fly-ins and air displays to keep the spirit of this great field alive.

The superb memorial to the 453rd BG At Old Buckenham is patterned after the tail-fin of a B24 Liberator.

Old Buckenham as it is today, a haven for light aircraft. Note the (theoretically) portable Control Tower.

Old Buckenham Operational History

Unit	Aircraft Type	Resident	Role
453rd BG (US 8th AF) 732nd, 733rd, 734th, 735th Bomb sqns	B24H, J, L, M Liberator	Dec 43-May 45	Heavy day bombing

Old Buckenham Plan

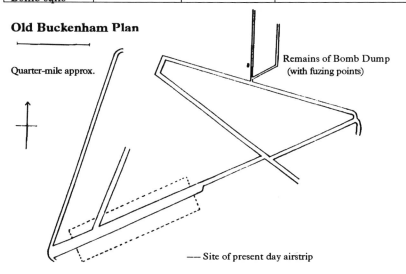

Quarter-mile approx.

Remains of Bomb Dump (with fuzing points)

—— Site of present day airstrip

(Reproduced from 1996 Landranger 144 1:50000 map by permission of Ordnance Survey on behalf of the Controller of Her Majesty's Stationery Office, Crown Copyright Licence MC99/281)

Oulton

Oulton airfield opened in 1940, but owes much of its fame to an older structure nearby. This is magnificent Blickling Hall - now a National Trust property - which provided opulent accommodation for Officers and NCOs throughout the war. Oulton was initially a satellite to Horsham St Faith (now Norwich Airport), and hosted a variety of light-bomber squadrons mainly operating the Blenheim.

By September 1942 the site had become a satellite to Swanton Morley, a move that saw the arrival of 88 sqn and its pugnacious Bostons. This unit conducted a wide variety of operations, including propaganda leaflet drops and no less than four attacks on the enemy vessel *Neumark*. However, they are best remembered for participating in the low-level daylight raid on the Philips works at Eindhoven, 6th December 1942.

September 1943 saw another change, as Oulton was transferred to the control of 100 Group, becoming a satellite to Foulsham. This entailed temporary closure so that the all-grass field could be upgraded to accept heavy bombers. The work was completed by May 1944, whereupon both RAF and USAAF specialist radio-countermeasures units arrived to conduct their highly secret war. Among the operations conducted was an investigation into the possible radio-control equipment behind the latest Nazi terror weapon, the V2 rocket.

Post-war, Oulton passed to Maintenance Command, and was used to store surplus Mosquito aircraft until closure in 1947. Today, in addition to a healthy number of surviving structures, the site is marked by a rare (in Norfolk) RAF memorial, and its history is told in a special display in the grounds of Blickling Hall. Blickling is always worth a visit, but to the aviation enthusiast is at its best when hosting one of its highly atmospheric Hot Air Balloon festivals.

As on many other former airfields, Oulton's runways owe their survival to their usefulness as foundations for poultry sheds.

Part of Oulton's Technical Site survives in agricultural use. Here, a Flight Office is just visible beyond the trees, along with two large Nissen-style General Purpose huts.

Oulton Operational History

Unit	Aircraft Type	Resident	Role
114 sqn	Blenheim IV	Aug 40-Mar 41	Light bombing
18 sqn	Blenheim IV	Apr 41-Jul 41	Light bombing
139 sqn	Blenheim IV	Jul 41-Sep 41	Anti-shipping patrol
18 sqn	Blenheim IV	Nov 41-Dec 41	Light bombing
59 sqn	Hudson GR.?	Dec 41	Anti-shipping patrol
139 sqn	Blenheim IV, Hudson III	Dec 41-Feb 42	Anti-shipping patrol
1428 Flt	Hudson III	Dec 41-May 42	Conversion to Hudson
139 sqn	Blenheim V, Mosquito IV	Jun 42-Aug 42	Light bombing
236 sqn	Beaufighter Ic	Jul 42-Sep 42	Anti-shipping strike
88 sqn	Boston III, IIIa	Sep 42-Mar 43	Light bombing
21 sqn	Ventura I, II	Apr 43-Sep 43	Light bombing
1699 Flt	Fortress I, II, III (B17E, F, G) Liberator VI (B24H)	May 44-Jun 44	Heavy bomber conversion
214 sqn	Fortress IIa, III	May 44-Jul 45	Radio counter-measures

803rdBS/ 36thBG (USAAF)	B17F, G Flying Fortress B24H, J, M Liberator	May 44-Aug 44	Radio counter-measures
223 sqn	Fortress IIa, III Liberator IV	Aug 44-Jul 45	Radio counter-measures
274 MU	Mosquito	Nov 45-Nov 46	Storage

Notes: Horsa gliders were stored at Oulton from April-September 1943.
Oulton's Station Flight comprised Airspeed Oxford and DH Tiger Moth.

Oulton Plan

Quarter-mile approx

Key

1. Bomb Dump
2. Squadron Office
3. WT/Bowser Store
4. Crew Locker & Drying Room
5. Main Stores
6. General Purpose Huts
7. Flight Office
8. T2 Hangar

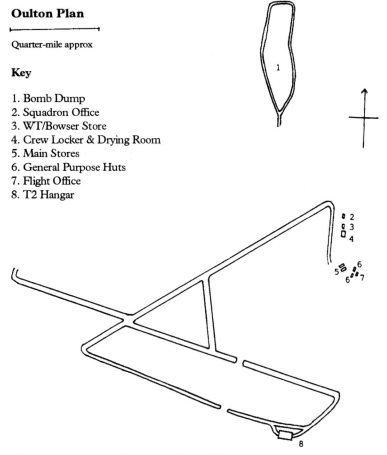

(Reproduced from 1996 Landranger 144 1:50000 map by permission of Ordnance Survey on behalf of the Controller of Her Majesty's Stationery Office, Crown Copyright Licence MC99/281)

Above: Memorials at RAF sites are comparatively rare. Oulton is a pleasing exception.

Left: The memorial to the 'Rackheath Aggies', located in the heart of the modern Industrial estate.

Rackheath

Like most of the airfields encircling the City of Norwich, Rackheath was built for the USAAF opening in March 1944 as Station 145. The only unit to occupy the site was the Liberator-equipped 467th Bomb Group, which under the exacting command of Colonel Albert Shower was to develop a most formidable reputation.

Beginning on 10th April 1944, the 'Rackheath Aggies' conducted 212 missions, eventually achieving the highest rate of bombing accuracy in the 8th Air Force. One of its aircraft, an H-model named 'Witchcraft', completed 130 combat sorties to become the longest-serving B24 in the entire 'Mighty Eighth'. A highlight among the 467th's varied missions was 11th June, a low-level strike on the strategic bridge at Blois-St-Denis. At the War's end the 467th was given the honour of leading the Victory Flypast over High Wycombe on May 13th 1945.

Inevitably, there were setbacks. One came on the night of 22nd April 1944, when Rackheath was targeted by a force of Me410 intruders. Two Liberators returning from an operation were shot down, and the airfield sustained some damage. Another bad day was December 29th, when thick fog enveloped the field and two B24s ran off the end of the runway, causing heavy casualties. However neither of these incidents, or the switch from strategic to tactical bombing in support of the Allied invasion, could dent the Aggies' success.

With the return of the 467th to the USA in July 1945, Rackheath was no longer required, and it was very quickly returned to agriculture. Today very little of the flying field is discernible, and the Technical Site has been swallowed up by an unusually pleasant and tidy industrial estate, although a few buildings remain. Among these, very much against the odds, is the Control Tower, and why no effort has been made to restore the building as a monument is an unfathomable mystery. Perhaps there is yet time for this oversight to be corrected.

Rackheath airfield has been thoroughly erased, as shown in this view across the site. The line of trees to the right parallels the former north-south runway.

Rackheath – Operational History

Unit	Aircraft Type	Resident	Role
467th BG **(US 8th AF)** 788th, 789th, 790th, 791st Bomb sqns	B24H, J, L, M Liberator	Mar 44-Jul 45	Heavy day bombing

Rackheath Plan

Quarter-mile approx

Key

1. Control Tower
2. Radar Workshop
3. NFE Store
4. Parachute Store
5. Main Workshops
6. Crew Locker & Drying Room
7. Trackway to Bomb Dump

(Reproduced from 1996 Landranger 144 1:50000 map by permission of Ordnance Survey on behalf of the Controller of Her Majesty's Stationery Office, Crown Copyright Licence MC99/281)

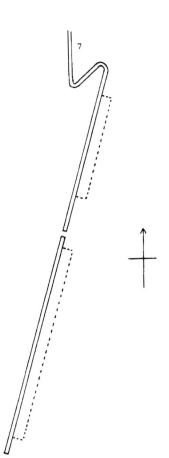

Weatherbeaten, but essentially intact, the Control Tower is today crammed with an assortment of rubbish.

The distinctive lop-sided shape of a Parachute Store, one of several buildings that survive from the former Technical Site at Rackheath.

Sculthorpe

Sculthorpe has such a deep-rooted association with the Cold-war era United States Air Force that it is easy to forget its origins in the Second World War. It was built in 1942, and opened in January 1943 as a satellite to West Raynham, under the control of 2 Group, RAF Bomber Command. 2 Group rapidly became part of the huge conglomeration of Allied air assets that was the 2nd Tactical Air Force. At the beginning of 1944 the airfield was reassigned to 100 Group.

By the middle of the year activity at Sculthorpe ceased, as the site was being upgraded to Very Heavy Bomber status in anticipation of USAAF B29 Superfortress units being committed to the assault on Nazi Germany. The runways were greatly lengthened, and many new buildings were erected including the Control Tower, as the field took on the shape it still retains today. In the event, the War ended before the B29s were required. In the immediate post-war period the site was used by a variety of American bomber units on 90-day rotations, including some operating the colossal B36 Peacemaker. In 1947 the USAAF became the USAF, an independent air arm.

Sculthorpe was officially handed over to the USAF in 1951, and for the next thirteen years saw a great variety of 'heavy metal' as a frontline base for the world's most powerful fighting force. But by 1964 the site was no longer needed and it was returned to the RAF, being placed on care and maintenance.

However, this was not the end, and in 1967 the USAF again took over, using Sculthorpe as a standby airfield through which detachments rotated just as they had done in the period just after World War 2. Indeed, I have clear memories from my youth of USAF bomber types glimpsed on the field as we drove past on our way to days out at Cromer and Sheringham. From the mid-1970s to the early 1980s a significant number of European fighters were flown into Sculthorpe for scrapping, and the site was also used by RAF and USAF units whose own local bases were being resurfaced. Regular activity at the field finally ceased in October 1983.

Sculthorpe officially closed on 2nd October 1992. The housing development built for American personnel and their families was famously sold off, as was the Technical Site. But once again this redoubtable airfield came back from the dead, and today it is part of STANTA and regularly used by Army Air Corps and RAF units on exercises. It is to be hoped that this magnificent aviation facility will continue to see use well into the future.

Sculthorpe – Operational History

Unit	Aircraft Type	Resident	Role
342 sqn	Boston IIIa	May 43-Jul 43	Light bombing
464 sqn	Ventura I, II Mosquito FB.VI	Jul 43-Dec 43	Light bombing
487 sqn	Ventura I, II Mosquito FB.VI	Jul 43-Dec 43	Light bombing
21 sqn	Mosquito FB.VI	Sep 43-Dec 43	Light bombing
214 sqn	Fortress II (B17F)	Jan 44-May 44	Radio countermeasures training
803rd BS (USAAF)	B17F, G Flying Fortress	Mar 44-May 44	Radio countermeasures training
91st SRG (US)	RB45C Tornado	May 51-Mar 55	Strategic reconnaissance
9th/67th ARS (US)	SB29 Superfortress SA16A Albatross	Aug 51-Oct 53	Air-sea rescue
60thTCW (US) 11th, 212th TCS	C119C Flying Boxcar	May 52-Dec 54	Transport
47thBG/BW (US) 84th, 85th, 86th, 422nd BS	B45A Tornado RB66B Destroyer	May 52-Jun 62	Light tactical bombing
19th TRS (US)	RB45C Tornado B66B Destroyer	Jun 52-Feb 59	Tactical reconnaissance
7554th TTF (US)	TB26C Invader L5 Sentinel	Jul 52-Jun 62	Target towing
49th ADCF	L20A Beaver, T33A	Apr 54-Jun 56	Communications/training
47th OS (US)	C47 Dakota, T29A, T33A, L20A Beaver C119G Flying Boxcar	Dec 54-Feb 58	Transport/ comms/training
420th ARS (US)	KB29P, KB50D, J Superfortress	Jan 56-Mar 64	Air-to-air refuelling
78th FBS (US)	F84F Thunderstreak	Apr 57-Sep 57	Fighter squadron

Base Flt (US)	C47 Dakota, T29A, T33A	Feb 58-Jun 62	Training/medevac
7375th SG (US)	C47 Dakota	Jun 62-Jun 64	Communications flights
28th WRS (US)	WB5OD Superfortress	Aug 62-Dec 62	Weather roconnaissance

Notes: Horsa gliders were stored at Sculthorpe from 1942-43.

Among the USAF units rotating through Sculthorpe from 1949-51 were the 92nd BG (B29); 43rd BG (B50); 2nd, 22nd, 97th & 301st BGs.

Units to use Sculthorpe while their home airfields were re-surfaced were:

July 78 – May 79: 55, 57, 100 sqns; 231, 232OCUS (EX-Marham)

May 82 – Dec 82: 6, 41, 54 sqns (ex-Coltishall)

June 83 – Oct 83: 48th TFW USAF (ex-Lakenheath)

Sculthorpe Plan

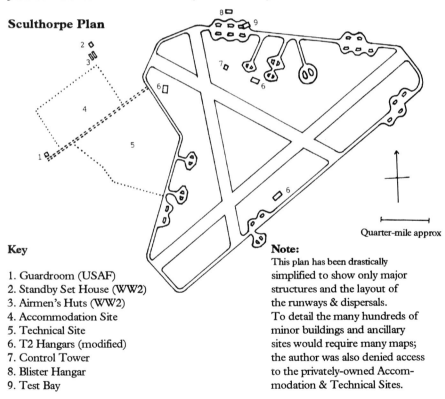

Quarter-mile approx

Key

1. Guardroom (USAF)
2. Standby Set House (WW2)
3. Airmen's Huts (WW2)
4. Accommodation Site
5. Technical Site
6. T2 Hangars (modified)
7. Control Tower
8. Blister Hangar
9. Test Bay

Note:

This plan has been drastically simplified to show only major structures and the layout of the runways & dispersals. To detail the many hundreds of minor buildings and ancillary sites would require many maps; the author was also denied access to the privately-owned Accommodation & Technical Sites.

Sculthorpe's wartime origins are discernible in this view of the former Accommodation Site, with the Standby Set House (behind the trees) and a pair of Airmen's huts (right). The other buildings date from the USAF's Cold-War occupation of the site, as does the basketball court.

This rare Blister hangar is another survivor from Sculthorpe's World War 2 service. The Control Tower visible in the distance gives an impression of the size of this huge airfield. This photo was taken from the short public footpath on the northern edge of the site, once a planespotter's paradise.

The magnificent Accommodation Blocks built post-war by the Americans are now in private hands, and their current use is a closely-guarded secret.

Sculthorpe's Control Tower was built right at the end of World War 2, and signifies the field's upgrading to Very Heavy Bomber Status.

Seething

Seething was one of the Norfolk airfields specifically constructed for the US 8th Air Force, this being done in 1942-43. The 448th Bomb Group, flying Liberators, conducted their first mission on 2nd December 1943, just three weeks after arriving in England. On 4th January 1944 they had a taste of the brutal nature of the daylight bombing campaign, losing four aircraft during a raid on Kiel.

Late in the evening of 22nd April, exhausted crews returning from a mission to the Hamm marshalling yards were 'bounced' by Me410 intruders. Two B24s were shot down with three more being destroyed on Seething's runways - a graphic illustration of the carnage a well-planned intruder could wreak.

Even as the European war headed towards its conclusion the 448th continued to suffer; on 4th April 1945 three B24s were lost in a determined attack by rare, but deadly, Me262 jet fighters. At the close of hostilities the 448th had sustained 101 losses in 262 operations - a very high rate indeed.

From September 1945 Seething served unglamorously but necessarily as a disposal centre for surplus bombs, finally being sold off in 1959. Since then the site has been owned by the Waveney Flying Group, and remains a very active light aviation concern. It was for many years a regular air display venue, but tragedy revisited the field in 1971 when famed pilot Neville Browning crashed and was killed while flying a Zlin aircraft. More recently, the Control Tower has been superbly restored to serve as a museum and memorial dedicated to the brave men of the 448th.

Seething's Control Tower, now beautifully restored as a museum and memorial dedicated to the 448th BG.

Seething – Operational History

Unit	Aircraft Type	Resident	Role
448thBG **(US 8thAF)** 712th, 713th, 714th, 715th Bomb sqns	B24H, J, L, M Liberator	Oct 42-Jun 45	Heavy day bombing

Seething – Plan

Quarter-mile approx

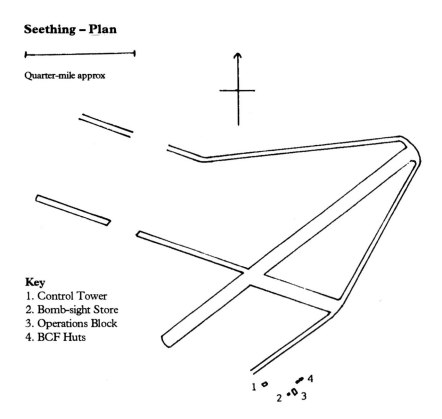

Key
1. Control Tower
2. Bomb-sight Store
3. Operations Block
4. BCF Huts

(Reproduced from 1996 Landranger 144 1:50000 map by permission of Ordnance Survey on behalf of the Controller of Her Majesty's StationeryOffice, Crown Copyright Licence MC99/281)

The Operations Block is well preserved in agricultural use.

Seething today is not just a light aircraft strip. Part of the site, close to the museum, is used by the Norwich Astronomy Group.

Ghost of a field: Seething's north-south runway has been completely removed, but its outline is preserved in the modern pattern of fields.

Shipdham

Built 1941-42, Shipdham occupies a seminal position in the history of Norfolk airfields. In August 1942 it became USAAF Station 115, the first location in the county to be used by the 'Mighty Eighth'. By October the 44th Bomb Group - the 'Flying Eightballs' - had arrived to inaugurate B24 Liberator operations from the UK. They carried out their first mission on 7th November, beginning a long and distinguished combat history that encompassed 343 operations with no less than six Marks of Consolidated's gloriously ugly, slab-sided heavy bomber.

The 44th gained its first Distinguished Unit Citation on 14th May 1944, when it alone conducted a mission to Kiel. Originally a full Combat Wing was slated for the raid, but poor weather led to the decision to scrub the operation. However, the abort message never reached Shipdham. Out of 17 aircraft dispatched, five were shot down and a sixth was forced to ditch on the way home. On the credit side, 21 enemy fighters were claimed by the 44th's gunners. Later in the year the 44th detached to North Africa to join the 15th AF, and while there participated in the legendary Plœsti raid, earning a second DUC.

However, it was not all glory for the 44th, as on the memorable date of 1st April 1944 it was one of the Groups inadvertently to bomb Schaffhausen in Switzerland, in the mistaken belief that they were over Ludwigshafen in Germany. This blip did little to dent the 44th's reputation, though, and at the War's end they had racked up one of the highest mission totals by a B24 Group, losing 153 aircraft in the process.

Post-war, Shipdham had an interesting history, becoming a prisoner-of-war camp until 1947. The site lingered until being sold off in 1963, and there its story might have ended had not the Shipdham Aero Club secured the northern side of the airfield and part of the main runway. Today the field is a haven for light aircraft, perhaps best known for its autogyro-themed special events. Rather less fortunate has been the former Technical Site, which has been swallowed up by what must be the tawdriest and most depressing industrial estate in creation. Amid piles of scrap metal and general detritus, only the hangars and the MT Section remain in reasonable order, with other key buildings descending into ruin.

Shipdham – Operational History

Unit	Aircraft Type	Resident	Role
44th BG (US 8thAF) 66th, 67th, 68th, 506th Bomb sqns	B24D, E, H, J, L, M Liberator	Oct 42-Jun 45	Heavy day bombing

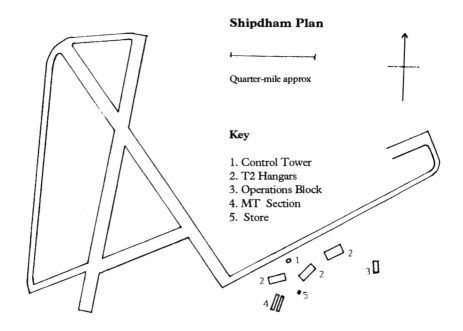

Shipdham Plan

Quarter-mile approx

Key

1. Control Tower
2. T2 Hangars
3. Operations Block
4. MT Section
5. Store

(Reproduced from 1996 Landranger 144 1:50000 map by permission of Ordnance Survey on behalf of the Controller of Her Majesty's StationeryOffice, Crown Copyright Licence MC99/281)

A Piper Pawnee glider tug taxis along the historic main runway at Shipdham. Clearly visible in the background are the remains of the Control Tower and the roofs of two hangars. (Foreshortening by the zoom lens makes the cranes seem more of a hazard than they really are.)

From a distance the Control Tower looks reasonably intact, but this view clearly shows the desperate state the building has fallen into.

One of the better-preserved buildings at Shipdham, the Motor Transport Section.

Snetterton Heath

World War 2 bombers were not, in the main, elegant-looking aircraft, but the B17 Flying Fortress was an exception to this rule. This was perhaps one reason why in fame it overshadowed the B24 Liberator. Beginning life way back in 1935 as the Boeing Model 299 - the first four-engined American 'heavy' - the B17 was the weapon with which the 8th Air Force inaugurated daylight operations over Europe in 1942. The theory that a heavily-armed, disciplined bomber formation was invulnerable to attack was to be comprehensively disproved by the skilled fighter pilots of the Luftwaffe, not to mention the deadly accurate Flak units, and it was only after a bitter war of attrition that the daylight campaign was ultimately vindicated.

One B17 Group that was to suffer particular hardships was the 96th, based at Snetterton Heath. Built 1942-43, Snetterton was originally intended for the RAF, but became USAAF Station 138. The 96th already had some combat experience when they moved into the site from Essex in July 1943. On August 17th they took part in the epic mission against Regensburg, gaining a Distinguished Unit Citation. But from then on things started to go wrong.

October 14th saw seven aircraft lost in the attack on one of the 8th AF's most formidable targets, Schweinfurt. Then, in a horrific span from April to June 1944, the 96th lost 100 aircraft, including ten during a disastrous attack on Rostock on April 11th. Ironically, the 96th gained its second DUC for a 'Shuttle' mission to Poznan in Poland just two days previously. By the War's end the 96th had lost 189 aircraft over 316 operations - the highest rate in the Eighth Air Force.

Somewhat surprisingly, this battered and exhausted unit stayed on in England after the end of hostilities. They ferried food supplies to Holland, and carried out training and transport flights throughout newly-liberated Europe. They did not return to the US until December 1945.

In 1952 Snetterton was privately purchased, and work began to develop part of the field into a motor racing circuit. Motor sport has thrived there ever since, and race days, with the added pleasure of helicopters and light aircraft, bring life to the historic site. Elsewhere, a significant number of dispersed buildings survive in industrial use, slightly tarnished monuments to the sacrifices made for freedom all those years ago.

Snetterton Heath – Operational History

Unit	Aircraft Type	Resident	Role
386th BG (US 8thAF) 552nd, 553rd, 554th, 555th Bomb sqns	B26B, C Marauder	Jun 43	Medium bombing
96th BG (US 8thAF) 337th, 338th, 339th, 413th Bomb sqns	B17F, G Flying Fortress	Jul 43-Dec 45	Heavy day bombing

Snetterton Heath Plan

Quarter-mile approx

Key

1. High-level Water Tank
2. Domestic Site (Nissens)
3. T2 Hangars
4. Workshop
5. General Purpose Huts
6. Administration Building
7. Double Gunnery Trainer
8. Electrical Sub-station
9. Single Gunnery Trainer
10. Instructional Building
11. Main Workshops

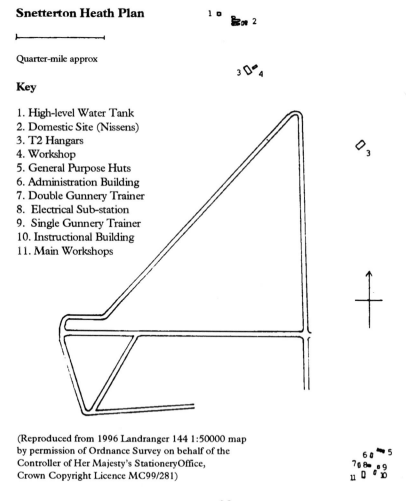

(Reproduced from 1996 Landranger 144 1:50000 map by permission of Ordnance Survey on behalf of the Controller of Her Majesty's StationeryOffice, Crown Copyright Licence MC99/281)

The motor racing circuit at Snetterton utilises much of the airfield's concrete runways and taxiways.

This Free Gunnery Trainer is one of several well-preserved buildings at the south (Eccles) Technical Site.

Right: Silent Sentinel. Pictured on a murky autumn day, this high-level water tank marks the location of the northerly domestic site. Snetterton is noteworthy for the extreme dispersal of its various sub-sites, to the extent that it was known in official documents as 'Snetterton Heath & Eccles'. Extensive roadworks have further fragmented what remains of this significant airfield.

Swannington

Construction work began on the airfield at Swannington (known to locals as Haveringland) in 1942, but protracted delays meant that the site did not open until spring 1944, making it the last of Norfolk's RAF airfields to come into operation. It was immediately assigned to 100 Group, and hosted two squadrons operating an aircraft type for which any and all superlatives are inadequate: the De Havilland DH98 Mosquito.

Famous for its mostly wooden construction, the Mosquito was essentially a private venture, and it stunned the sceptical authorities with its phenomenal speed and maoeuvrability. It was also one of the most beautiful aircraft ever built, thus proving the old aviation maxim, 'if it looks right, it is right'. The Mosquito fulfilled almost every imaginable role in World War 2, setting a standard for versatility that will probably never be equalled.

85 and 157 squadrons mainly conducted night intruder missions, but they also took on V1 Flying Bombs, for which purpose they detached to Kent. Later, refined tactics and improved Air Interception radar saw the 'Mossies' working within RAF bomber streams, picking off opposing night-fighters with lethal accuracy.

The other aircraft type associated with Swannington is equally legendary: the Supermarine Spitfire. Operated by 229 and 451 (Australian) squadrons, in its Griffon-engined MkXVI form the Spit was a long way from R. J. Mitchell's original design, but there is no mistaking the graceful form of history's most famous fighter. The Swannington-based Spits conducted daylight bomber escort, signifying the increasing Allied air superiority as Bomber Command moved beyond night raids.

The Mosquito squadrons were active during the mission to Kiel, 2nd-3rd of May 1945, the final Bomber Command operation against Nazi Germany. Activity at Swannington rapidly dwindled to nothing, although surplus equipment was stored at the site in the immediate post-war years. Sold off in 1957, the site has fared surprisingly well in agricultural and light industrial use. The growl of heavy lorries has replaced the roar of Griffon and Merlin engines, but there is still a fair bit to see by following the triangle of minor roads immediately north of Swannington village.

Swannington – Operational History

Unit	Aircraft Type	Resident	Role
157 sqn	Mosquito II, XIX, XXX	May 44-Aug 45	Night intruder missions
85 sqn	Mosquito XIII, XVII, XXX	May 44-Jun 45	Night intruder missions
229 sqn	Spitfire XVIe	Nov 44-Dec 44	Fighter/escort
451 sqn	Spitfire XVI	Feb 45-Apr 45	Fighter/escort

A Norfolk speciality, the round-towered church in the mid-distance must have been a comfort to aircrews as they taxied along the perimeter track, and a welcome sight for those fortunate enough to return to Swannington. The trees on the right mark the extremity of the main runway.

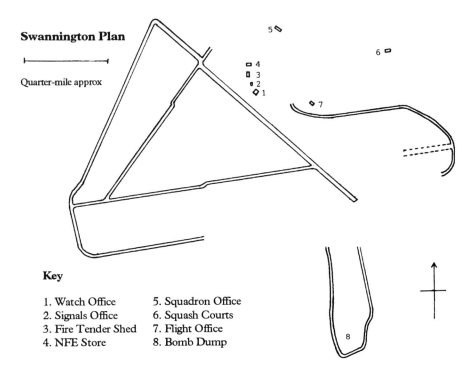

Swannington Plan

Quarter-mile approx

5

6

4
3
2
1

7

Key

1. Watch Office
2. Signals Office
3. Fire Tender Shed
4. NFE Store
5. Squadron Office
6. Squash Courts
7. Flight Office
8. Bomb Dump

(Reproduced from 1996 Landranger 144 1:50000 map by permission of Ordnance Survey on behalf of the Controller of Her Majesty's Stationery Office, Crown Copyright Licence MC99/281)

From the days of World War 1 to the end of World War 2, squash courts were considered an important part of airfield domestic sites. Many examples survive, with Swannington's one of the best-preserved.

Lost in the woods, the ruin of the former communal site at Thorpe Abbotts is a ghostly reminder of the 'Bloody Hundredth'.

Thorpe Abbotts

In any armed conflict, there are certain units that somehow transcend the simple history of men and machines to attain the status of legend. If one thinks of the American 8th Air Force in World War 2, two units spring instantly to mind: the Bassingbourn-based 91st Bomb Group, home of the 'Memphis Belle' and Tony Starcer's fabulous nose art; and from Thorpe Abbotts, the 100th BG, aka the 'Bloody Hundredth'.

Despite its reputation as a jinxed outfit, the 100th's overall loss rate was not significantly worse than that of other Groups, though at 177 aircraft from 306 missions, with over 700 lives lost, it was tragic enough. Perhaps it was the fact that many of their losses came during some of the Eighth's most gruelling air battles that gave the 100th's story its particular poignancy, and made it symbolic of the USAAF's daylight war of attrition against Nazi Germany.

Thorpe Abbotts was built in 1942 as a satellite to Horsham, with the first elements of the 100th arriving in June 1943, and the first mission being flown on the 25th. On 17th August the Group took part in the infamous 'Shuttle' raid on the twin targets of Regensburg and Schweinfurt. Bringing up the rear of the massive bomber formation headed for Regensburg, the 100th found itself without fighter escort and at the mercy of the Luftwaffe. Seven B17s were lost on the approach to the target, and two more crash-landed en route to the distant havens in North Africa. It was a grim portent of what was to follow, although morale was somewhat boosted by the award of a Distinguished Unit Citation.

In one dreadful week during October, the 100th lost a further 21 aircraft. Then, in March 1944 the Group carried out no less than three attacks on Berlin, earning their second DUC but suffering more casualties. The 11th of September saw eleven aircraft lost during an attack on Merseburg, and added to this was a high rate of accidents such as the one on 7th November when a flare-gun exploded aboard a B17G during a practice mission, causing the plane to break up over Felixstowe. At one point even the airfield itself got involved: on 5th January 1945 two aircraft collided over Thorpe Abbotts, one falling on the Bomb Dump and detonating a considerable amount of ordnance. Such mishaps were part and parcel of the frantic air operations over East Anglia, but for the 100th they merely served to emphasise an already grim reputation.

The 100th's vicious campaign finally ended on 20th April, after which the Group lingered in the UK before finally returning to the US in December. Thorpe Abbotts reverted to RAF control, but the field was never used again and was sold off in 1956. Agriculture took over, but the Control Tower survived and as time passed, and the 100th's reputation grew, it became the focus of renewed interest. In the 1980s a determined campaign came to fruition and the Tower was restored as the centrepiece of the 100th BG Memorial Museum, now a place of pilgrimage for all those interested in the heroism of the past. The 'Bloody Hundredth's' legacy also lives on not too far away at Mildenhall, Suffolk, from where its modern-day successor, the 100th Air Refuelling Wing, operates its majestic KC135 Stratotankers.

Thorpe Abbotts – Operational History

Unit	Aircraft Type	Resident	Role
100th BG (US 8th AF) 349th, 350th, 351st, 418th Bomb sqns	B17F, G Flying Fortress	Jun 43-Dec 45	Heavy day bombing

Thorpe Abbotts Plan

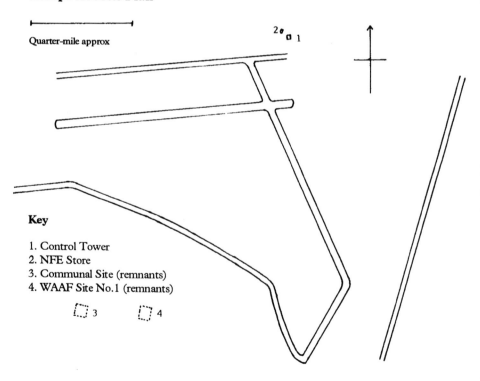

Quarter-mile approx

Key

1. Control Tower
2. NFE Store
3. Communal Site (remnants)
4. WAAF Site No.1 (remnants)

Well-preserved stretch of the northern perimeter track - heavily-laden B17s once picked their way along this route.

The restored Control Tower looks out on a field now fully returned to agriculture. Additional buildings, rescued from other sites, have been added to make up the Museum complex.

Tibenham

Purpose-built in 1942-43 as USAAF Station 124, Tibenham occupied a site once used by the Royal Flying Corps in World War 1, and like almost all Norfolk airfields was known by a different name to locals, in this case Tivetshall.

Unsurprisingly, it was a B24 Liberator Group, the 445th, that took up residence at Tibenham. From their first mission - a raid on Kiel, 13th December 1943 - the 445th were fairly successful, and they were awarded a Distinguished Unit Citation for their part in the Gotha raid of 24th February 1944. However, later that year things were to take a dramatic downward turn.

The target on 27th September was Kassel, site of the Henschel engine factory. The 445th dispatched 37 Liberators for this mission, but thanks to a navigational error the Group lost contact with the main bomber force, and ended up hitting the wrong target. On the return leg the Group was 'bounced' by a huge force of enemy fighters, and virtually obliterated. Twenty-five aircraft went down almost immediately, two more crash-landed in France and a further three crashed in England. Even the seven aircraft that made it home were severely damaged. The loss - 30 aircraft and 236 aircrew missing - was the worst suffered in one day by any 8th Air Force Bomber Group.

Unbelievably, the 445th rebounded from this disaster, and they went on to conduct a total of 282 operations. They built up a formidable reputation for the accuracy of their attacks, and their success in dropping food supplies to the French Resistance saw the Group awarded the Croix de Guerre. By July 1945, their bitter war was finally over; the 445th had returned Stateside.

Reverting to RAF control, Tibenham remained active although military aircraft were no longer part of the equation. The site served as a Reception Centre for troops returning from overseas, then as a Food Storage Depot. In 1955 the field was expanded for possible use by the USAF, but nothing came of this and Tibenham closed in 1959. Almost immediately the Norfolk Gliding Club moved in, and ever since their graceful machines have soared over the field's well-preserved runways. Today, gliding competitions provide the only drama - a fitting symbol of the peace hard-won years before.

Tibenham – Operational History

Unit	Aircraft Type	Resident	Role
445thBG (US 8thAF) 700th, 701st, 702nd, 703rd Bomb sqns	B24H, J, L, M, Liberator	Nov 43-May 45	Heavy day bombing

A glider settles gracefully onto Tibenham's well-maintained runways. The present-day airstrip, with its assortment of aircraft sheds, is well illustrated in this shot.

Tibenham Plan

Quarter-mile approx

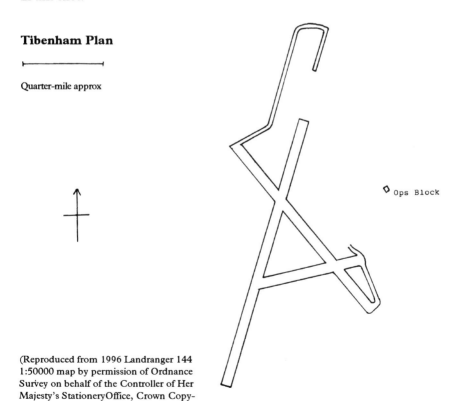

Ops Block

(Reproduced from 1996 Landranger 144 1:50000 map by permission of Ordnance Survey on behalf of the Controller of Her Majesty's StationeryOffice, Crown Copyright Licence MC99/281)

Watton

Few airfields can lay claim to as varied a history as Watton. It was built in 1937-38 to the typical expansion-era pattern, and anyone familiar with such stations as Bircham Newton and West Raynham could find their way round here blindfold. The ubiquitous and long-suffering Blenheim squadrons were the site's first residents, and the appalling rates of attrition they endured are starkly illustrated by the story of 82 sqn.

On 17th May 1940 this unit sent 12 aircraft to attack German armoured columns advancing across France, but they never got there. The squadron was 'bounced' by Bf109 fighters and eleven Blenheims were shot down with the loss of 33 aircrew. The only plane to survive was that piloted by 82's commander, the Earl of Brandon. Through sheer will-power, the Earl was able to reconstitute his unit, but on August 13th there was another catastrophe. The target was an airfield in Denmark, and of eleven aircraft carrying out the attack five were lost to flak over the target, and the remaining six were downed by 109s on the return trip. Such disasters heralded the end of the RAF's day bombing campaign, but the Blenheim continued to suffer badly until it was finally withdrawn from frontline service.

By 1942 operational units at Watton had mostly given way to training units, and then in July 1943 the life of the airfield changed abruptly as it was upgraded to Heavy Bomber status and became USAAF Station 376. However, Watton was to be no ordinary 'Mighty Eighth' repository: the south-west corner of the site was massively expanded and developed to accommodate the 3rd Strategic Air Deport.

3rd SAD had hardly any aircraft of its own, but saw a constant stream of visitors in the form of B24 Liberator bombers. The unit's task was to supply, service and repair B24s for the 8th AF's Second Bombardment Division, which at peak strength operated some 1,000 Liberators. 3rd SAD was also tasked with salvaging bombers that had crashed in the UK - a very depressing duty. At its peak, 3rd SAD was so large it was a station in its own right, named Neaton by the Americans. Sadly, nothing survives today, as the site was obliterated in the building of HMP Wayland.

Meanwhile, at Watton itself, some unusual units took up residence. Briefly, the black-painted Liberators of the hush-hush Special Operations Group - the 'Carpetbaggers' - were based here. They conducted a variety of clandestine operations in support of the French Resistance. Then came the 802nd Reconnaissance Group, operating a variety of aircraft including the sleek and skittish Martin B26 Marauder - a rare sight at Norfolk airfields. This unit initially conducted weather reconnaissance, but later progressed to photographic work and ultimately supported major raids by dropping 'Chaff' - the American term for 'Window'.

After the War, Watton entered another very different phase of its history. Today, Electronic Warfare, in particular the monitoring and disruption of enemy communications, is a vital element of air warfare, but in 1946 it was still a relatively new concept. In that year the Central Signals Establishment took up residence, and for over 20 years a dazzling variety of aircraft types would fly from Watton, developing and deploying radars and radios, electronic intelligence-gathering equipment and electronic countermeasures.

Watton went into decline in the 1970s, being used only by University Air Squadrons and transports operating into the nearby Stanford Training Area. Handed over to the Army in 1982, the flying field is now officially part of STANTA, and still regularly hosts airmobile exercises. Parts of the field have been developed to simulate a variety of battlefield environments, providing realistic Air Assault scenarios. The rest of the site has experienced mixed fortunes: the NAAFI and accommodation blocks have passed into civilian industrial use and are well preserved. However, the Technical Site is in the hands of a private developer and thus its future is questionable.

Watton – Operational History

Unit	Aircraft Type	Resident	Role
34 sqn	Blenheim I	Feb 39-Aug 39	Bombing training
21 sqn	Blenheim I, IV	Mar 39-Dec 41	Coastal patrol
82 sqn	Blenheim I, IV	Aug 39-Mar 42	Day bombing/ Coastal patrol
18 sqn	Blenheim IV	May 40	Day bombing
105 sqn	Blenheim IV	Jul 40-Oct 40	Day bombing
61 sqn	Hampden I	Apr 41	Medium bombing (special ops)
90 sqn	Fortress I (B17C)	May 41	Day bombing
No8 BAT flt	Blenheim I	Dec 41-Jan 42	Blind landing training
17(Pilot) AFU	Master II	Feb 42-Jun 43	Advanced pilot training
3rd SAD (USAAF)	C45 Expeditor UC64 Norseman Oxford II	Jul 43-Aug 45	Bomber repair/ overhaul/ salvage (B24s)
SOG (USAAF) 36th BS, 406th BS	B24D Liberator	Feb 44-Apr 44	Special ops (Resistance support)
802ndRG/25thBG (US 8thAF) 652nd, 653rd, 654th Bomb sqns	B24D, H Liberator B17G Flying Fortress Mosquito XVI B26G Marauder L5 Sentinel	Apr 44-Jul 45	Reconnaissance/ Countermeasures

Central Signals Establishment (aka Radio Warfare Establishment)	Lancaster I, III Halifax III B17G Flying Fortress MosquitoB.XVI, NF30 Spitfire Vb Wellington X Dominie, Oxford II Anson I, XII, 19 Proctor C2, Lincoln B2	Sep 45-Aug 52	Electronic warfare
527 sqn	Wellington X Oxford II Spitfire Vb Mosquito NF30 Dominie I Harvard T2	Nov 45-Apr 46	Radar/radio calibration
751 sqn	Anson I Oxford I	Mar 47-Sep 47	Radar trials
CSE Development sqn	Lincoln B2 Varsity CanberraB2, B6, T4 Meteor T7, NF11, NF12	Aug 50-Jan 62	Electronics evaluation
192 sqn	Lincoln B2 Anson C19 Mosquito PR34 Washington (B29) Canberra B2, B6 Varsity T1 Comet C2 (R)	Jul 51- Aug 58	Electronic intelligence gathering
199 sqn	Lincoln B2 Mosquito NF36	Jul 51-Apr 52	Radio-countermeasures training
751 sqn (RN)	Mosquito FB6, PR34 Sea Mosquito TR33 Sea Fury FB11 Firefly AS5, AS6 Sea Venom 21	Dec 51-Sep 57	Electronics trials/training
527 sqn	Mosquito B35 Anson C19, Lincoln B2 Meteor NF11, NF14 Varsity T1 Canberra B2, PR7, T4	Aug 52-Aug 58	Radar/radio calibration

116 sqn	Anson C19 Lincoln B2 Valetta T4, Varsity T1 Hastings C1	Aug 52-Aug 58	Radar/radio calibration
815 sqn (RN)	Avenger AS5	Oct 54	Anti-submarine training
831 sqn (RN)	Avenger AS6 Gannet ECM4, ECM6 Sea Venom ECM21, ECM22	May 58-Jun 63	Electronic warfare
51 sqn	Canberra B2, B6, T4 Comet C2 (R)	Aug 58-Mar 63	Long-range reconnaissance
263 sqn	Bloodhound I	Jun 59-Jun 63	Airfield missile defence
151 sqn	Lincoln B2, Varsity T1, Hastings C2 Canberra B2, T4	Jan 62-May 63	Electronics development
97/831sqn (RAF/RN)	Varsity T1, Hastings C2 Canberra B2, B6	May 63-Jan 67	Electronics development
115 sqn	Valetta C1, Varsity T1 Argosy E1, Hastings T2	Oct 63-Apr 69	Radar/radio calibration
98 sqn	Canberra B2, T4	Oct 63-Apr 69	High altitude calibration
360sqn (RAF/RN)	Canberra B2, B6, T4, T17	Jan 67-Jul 67	Electronic countermeasures
361 sqn	Canberra T4, T17	Jan 67-Jul 67	Electronic countermeasures

These Robin sheds are among the many interesting smaller buildings still in situ on the main airfield site.

Watton Plan

Quarter-mile approx.

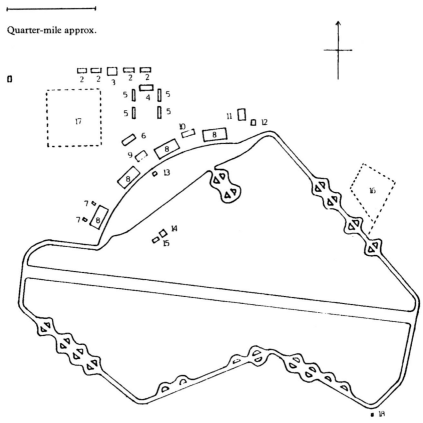

Key

1. Gymnasium	7. Transit Sheds	13. Watch Office (original)
2. H-Block Barracks	8. C-Type Hangars	14. Control Tower (modified)
3. NAAFI	9. Armoury & Photo. Section	15. Fire Section
4. Kestrel Club	10. Six-bay Tanker Shed	16. Bomb Dump
5. Barrack Blocks	11. Motor Transport Section	17. Site of Eastern Radar
6. Central Heating Station	12. Robin Sheds	18. Aircraft Test Butt

Note: This plan has been simplified to show only major buildings. The Technical Site in particular lacks detail because it proved impossible to contactthe current landowners and gain access.

Watton's original Watch Office was a concrete 'Fort' type, to drawing 207 of 1936.

The later Control Tower at Watton shows various stages of development during its operational life. The World War 2 building was augmented by a Cold War 'glasshouse' (drawing 5871c of 1955), a type still familiar at modern military airfields.

From 1956 part of the Watton site was used as a radar control centre for civilian and military traffic over East Anglia. Known as 'Eastern Radar', it finally ceased operations in 1992. Shown is one of the many buildings that formed the radar complex.

A classic H-block Barrack (actually a type L), built to a 1938 design. This is now the appropriately-named 'Ventura House'.

A view along the 'piano keys' at the western end of Watton's runway. Like most airfields that survived into the jet era, the original runway layout was abandoned in favour of a single, extended main.

Sealed up and largely forgotten, Watton's imposing C-type hangars face an uncertain future.

Wendling

Wendling - known locally as Beeston - was built for the 8th AF in 1942, and opened in August 1943. Its history is that of the only unit to operate from the field, the 392nd Bomb Group. This was the fourth B24 Liberator group to reach England, and the first to employ the H model of this famous bomber. The Group experienced a slow build-up in operations, being initially confined to diversionary attacks and then training flights while the other three 8th AF B24 groups were detached to North Africa. It was not until October '43 that the Group began its campaign in earnest, but on the 16th November it participated in a significant attack on the Heavy Water plant at Rjuken in Norway.

The 392nd went on to conduct 285 missions, dropping 17,500 tons of bombs and losing 184 aircraft - a significantly high loss rate. Seven B24s went down on the 24th February 1944 during an attack on the Gotha aircraft factory, although the Group's gunners claimed eight enemy fighters destroyed and the 392nd received a Distinguished Unit Citation for this raid. The worst day for the Group was 18th March '44, when the target was Frederichshafen. Two B24s collided over France, twelve were shot down by fighters and a further two force-landed in Switzerland.

John Ellis of the 577th sqn was one 392nd pilot whose name is remembered with particular reverence for an act of supreme self-sacrifice, on 12th August 1944. While forming up for a raid Ellis's B24 collided with a B17 over Hertfordshire. Ellis and his crew somehow steered the stricken bomber away from built-up areas, and it crashed near the A10 road with the loss of all on board. A memorial to this gallant crew was raised in Cheshunt library.

The 392nd left Wendling in June 1945, and the station was handed back to the RAF. Though it never again hosted flying units, the site lingered until November 1961, finally being sold off in 1963. Today, turkey sheds cover the runways and little remains, although parts of the dispersed accommodation site survive in reasonable condition. There is, however, a magnificent memorial to the 392nd in Beeston village, and a nearby microlight strip ensures the skies over Wendling are never totally silent.

Wendling – Operational History

Unit	Aircraft Type	Resident	Role
392nd BG (US 8thAF) 576th, 577th, 578th, 579th Bomb sqns	B24H, J, L, M Liberator	Aug 43-Jun 45	Heavy day bombing

Under a classic Norfolk sky, the one-time bomber base at Wendling is discernible only by the chicken sheds built on its old runways.

Wendling Plan

Quarter-mile approx

Key

1. Bomb Dump
2. Auto Repair Shop
3. Site No. 12
4. Part of Communal Site

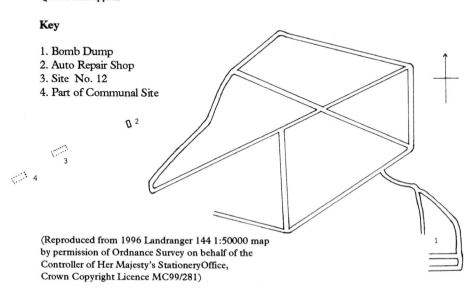

(Reproduced from 1996 Landranger 144 1:50000 map by permission of Ordnance Survey on behalf of the Controller of Her Majesty's StationeryOffice, Crown Copyright Licence MC99/281)

The former Auto Repair Shop lives on in appropriate style, now a spares/salvage centre devoted to Jaguar cars.

The remains of Wendling's Bomb Dump, now part of a small nature reserve.

Part of the Communal Site, with a very large, Nissen-style 'Romney' hut. These versatile buildings served as billets, dining halls and briefing rooms.

An impressive collection of rare Orlit huts comprising part of Site no. 12, not far from the present memorial in Beeston.

West Raynham

West Raynham was, and remains, a classic expansion-era airfield, complete with C-type hangars, H-block barracks and a palatial Officers' Mess. Officially opened in May 1939, the site had been used prior to this date for Operational Readiness exercises. Typically, resident squadrons in the early years of the war were Blenheim units, which attacked oil and communications targets, as well as enemy airfields, mostly by day. However, one Blenheim squadron - no. 101 - took part in a night raid on Mannheim, conducted in retaliation for the Luftwaffe attacks on Coventry and Southampton, but suffered heavy losses. The airfield itself was attacked on several occasions throughout 1940 and 1941.

In the autumn of 1942, 98 and 180 sqns became the first RAF units to operate the North American B25 Mitchell medium bomber. This pugnacious twin-engined type soon established a formidable reputation and is regarded today as one of the best bombers of World War 2. It served in every theatre of war although curiously, only the RAF operated it from British soil.

From May-Nov 1943 Raynham's grass runways were replaced by concrete, although unusually only two concrete runways were laid in contrast to the familiar A pattern. As the War drew to its close the second and most significant phase of the airfield's history began. In 1945 the RAF's Central Fighter Establishment and the Royal Navy's Air Fighting Development Unit arrived, and for the next 20 years West Raynham would see a bewildering variety of aircraft types as the Piston Era gave way to the Jet Age and these units plus others evaluated newly-introduced types and developed operational doctrines.

In the late 'sixties the airfield began to go into decline and from 1977 the unsettling silhouettes of Bloodhound missiles were the only things to be seen there. The Bloodhounds finally moved out in the late 1980s and Raynham closed in July 1994. It remains MOD property on a care and maintenance basis, but its long-term future is uncertain.

I have a very particular personal attachment to West Raynham airfield. From 1947-49 one Hugh McKenzie - a Glasgow native - conducted his National Service at the station, and while there he met and wooed a Norfolk girl, June Hill. Eventually they married and settled in King's Lynn, and one product of their union was a slightly freaky son who grew up with a passionate interest in aviation history. On June 1st 1994 that son was privileged to accompany his father to the official Closing Ceremony for West Raynham, and in October 2000 was able to take him back one more time in the course of researching this project. On which highly personal footnote, we take our leave of the major Norfolk airfields of World War 2.

West Raynham – Operational History

Unit	Aircraft Type	Resident	Role
101 sqn	Blenheim IV Wellington 1c	May 39-Jul 41	Day/night bombing
90 sqn	Blenheim I, IV	May 39-Sep 39	Bombing training
2 Grp TT flt	Blenheim I, Battle II, Lysander II, Tutor	Feb 40-Jan 42	Target towing
76 sqn	Anson I, Hampden I	Apr 40-May 40	Bombing training
139 sqn	Blenheim IV	May 40-Jun 40	Day bombing
18 sqn	Blenheim IV	Jun 40-Sep 40	Bombing training
90 sqn	Fortress I (B17C)	May 41-Jun 41	High altitude trials
1420 flt	Blenheim IV	Jul 41-Nov 41	Bombing training
114 sqn	Blenheim IV, V	Jul 41-Nov 42	Light day bombing
1482 sqn	Lysander II, Defiant TT.III Blenheim IV, V Martinet TT.I, Boston III, Ventura II, Mitchell II, Tomahawk II, Hurricane IV	Jan 42-Dec 43	Target towing/bombing practise
614 sqn	Blenheim IV	May 42-Jul 42	Night intruder attacks
18 sqn	Blenheim IV, Vd	Aug 42-Nov 42	Bombing training
180 sqn	Mitchell II	Sep 42-Oct 42	Medium bombing
98 sqn	Mitchell II	Sep 42-Oct 42	Medium bombing
342 sqn	Boston IIIa	Apr 43-May 43	Bombing training
141 sqn	Beaufighter VIf Mosquito II, FB.VI, NF30	Dec 43-Jul 45	Night intruder attacks
239 sqn	Mosquito II, FB.VI, NF30	Dec 43-Jul 45	Night intruder attacks
746 sqn (RN)	Firefly NF.I, NF.II Hellcat NF.II	May 45- Jan 46	Night fighter trials

CFE	Tempest II, V Spitfire IX, XIV, 21 MosquitoFB.VI, NF30, NF36 Hornet F1, F3 Meteor F4, F8, NF11, NF14 Vampire FB.I, FB.V Venom FB.1, NF3, F36A Sabre Hunter F1, F4, F6, Swift F1, F4 Javelin FAW1, FAW5, FAW8	Jul 45-Nov 62	Fighter trials/evaluation
NAFDU (aka 787 sqn RN)	Firefly FR4, NF1, NF5 Hellcat nf11 Firebrand F4 Sea Mosquito TR33 Sea Hornet NF21 Attacker F1, F2 Avenger AS4, Wyvern S4 Sea Vampire F20 Sea Hawk F1, FB3, FGA4 Sea Venom FAW21 Oxford I, Dominie I Gannet AS1	Nov 45-Jan 56	Fighter trials/evaluation
CFE Comms flt	Oxford II Anson C19, C21 Meteor T7	Dec 45-? 57	Communications
CFE TT flt	Martinet TT.III Mosquito B35 Balliol T2 Canberra T4, T11 Meteor T7	? 46–Apr 63	Target towing
FighterCmd Instrument Training sqn	Oxford II, Mosquito T3 Meteor T7, Vampire T11	Feb 50-Dec 52	Pilot/instructor rating
85 sqn	Javelin FAW8	Sep 60–Apr 63	Fighter (all weather)
54 sqn/ 4 sqn	Hunter FGA9	Aug 63-Jan 70	Ground attack/ Army support
1 sqn	Hunter FGA9	Aug 63-Jul 69	Ground attack

Kestrel Evaluation sqn	Kestrel	Oct 64-Dec 65	Trials of Hawker Kestrel
41 sqn	Bloodhound 2	Sep 65-Sep 70	Airfield missile defence
38Grp Comms flt	Auster AOP9	? 66-? 68	Communications
85 sqn	Canberra B2, T4, T19	Jan 72-Dec 75	Target facilities
100 sqn	Canberra B2, T4, T19	Feb 72-Jan 76	Target facilities
45 sqn	Hunter FGA9	Aug 72-Sep 72	Ground attack
85 sqn	Bloodhound 2	Dec 75-? 88	Airfield missile defence

Notes: While the CFE was very much a peacetime unit, it could still suffer significant operational attrition. The most dramatic example came in 1956 when six of the eight Hunters on a training flight crashed in thick fog while attempting to divert to Marham, resulting in one fatality.

The impressive, if utilitarian, Station Headquarters

121

West Raynham Plan

Quarter-mile approx.

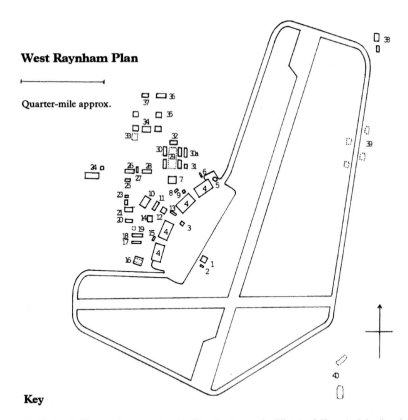

Key

1. Control Tower (post-war) 2. Fire Section 3. Watch Office (original) 4. C-type Hangars 5. Missile Dome Trainer 6. Oil Store 7. Main Stores and Intelligence Block 8. Dope Store 9. Lubricant Store 10. Air Ministry Works Dept. and Water Tower 11. Central Heating Station 12. Armoury & Photographic Section 13. Night Flying equipment Store 14. Main Workshops 15. Tanker Shed 16. Shooting Range 17. Motor Transport Shed 18. Motor Transport Shed 19. Fuel Store/Scrap Bins 20. Gas Decontamination Centre 21. Station Sick Quarters 22. Gas Decontamination Centre 23. Ambulance Station 24. Officers' Mess & Squash Courts 25. Guard Room 26. Station Headquarters 27. Chapel 28. Sergeants' Mess 29. Parade Ground 30. Barrack Blocks (4) 30a. Barrack Blocks (later Computer Training Centre) 31. Shop/Stores 32. NAAFI (later Kestrel Club) 33. Tennis Courts 34. Cookhouse/Restaurant & Cinema 35. H-Blocks 36. Motor Transport Section 37.Central Heating Station 38. Bloodhound Maintenance Section 39. Bloodhound Missile Pads 40. Incendiary/Pyrotechnic Store

(Reproduced from 1996 Landranger 144 1:50000 map by permission of Ordnance Survey on behalf of the Controller of Her Majesty's StationeryOffice, Crown Copyright Licence MC99/281)

Note: This plan has been simplified to show major structures & buildings of particular interest. For the time being, West Raynham is a perfectly preserved airfield with hundreds of buildings reflecting its almost sixty-year operational history.

The Chapel is one of the more unusual buildings to be found at Raynham.

Above: Vivid red Boston ivy adorns the No. 2 Hangar at West Raynham. The airfield's mothballed status has allowed once carefully-tended greenery to run riot.

Right: The Airmen's Restaurant was one of the centres of Station life. Its upper floor served ss a cinema.

Above: The acme of Watch Office/Control Tower development was drawing 294 of 1945, designed for Very Heavy Bomber stations. Only two examples survive, at Sculthorpe and West Raynham. Despite outward appearance, Raynham's tower has suffered severe damage and is in poor condition.

Left: Raynham's original Watch Office began life as a 'Fort' type but was modified to drawing 4698 of 1943.

A fine example of a six-bay Petrol Tanker Shed.

The Station Sick Quarters, to drawing 7503 of 1937, with its Decontamination Block visible behind.

The former Shooting Range at Raynham survives in exceptional condition.

For many years now, airfield defence has been in the hands of Rapier missile units. This futuristic structure was used to train Rapier crew, and makes an interesting comparison with the Dome Trainer at Langham.

Overgrown but otherwise intact, the Officers' Mess is a variation on the classic expansion-era drawing 2948 of 1934. Faint traces of wartime camouflage paint can still be seen on the exterior walls.

Shadow Fields - World War 2 Decoy Sites

In 1939, Colonel Sir John Turner took charge of one of history's most unusual military units. 'Col. Turner's Department', as it was known, oversaw the development of wartime deception, which in Britain was taken to extremes during World War 2. In the realm of aviation this involved the creation of dummy airfields in the vicinity of genuine operational stations - each real airfield would have at least one decoy, and some had several.

Decoy airfields came in two varieties - K sites were for daytime use, Q sites were for night operation, although many sites fulfilled both roles. 'Col. Turner's Department' drew heavily on the field of cinema, and the range of effects used was worthy of Hollywood, let alone Ealing. K sites employed fake fighters and bombers made of wood and canvas, while huge sheets of specially-painted canvas simulated the roofs of hangars. To enhance the effect, real aircraft - often impressed civilian biplanes - puttered about these sites, as did barely-roadworthy jeeps and tankers. At Q sites, mock flarepaths were laid out, and imitation runway lights were operated from remote bunkers which today are generally the only surviving remnants of such activity. There was even an elaborate system designed to simulate an aircraft taxiing at night. Sometimes the effect was a little too realistic - there are numerous instances of Allied aircraft coming to grief while attempting to land at imitation airfields.

The precise effectiveness of the K/Q sites is a subject of intense debate. Almost all were attacked at some point, demonstrating their realism. However, Luftwaffe documents secured after the war indicate the Germans very rapidly sussed the situation, and there is at least one recorded incident of dummy bombs being dropped on a dummy airfield. Once 'rumbled', many decoys were developed into full-blown airfields, as detailed elsewhere.

Airfields represented only part of the deception undertaken by 'Col. Turner's Department'. 'Starfish' sites involved the simulation of railway yards and sometimes entire towns with carefully-choreographed lighting effects. In the build-up to D-Day dummy gun-batteries, Army convoys and landing-craft were deployed in their hundreds. The whole subject of wartime decoys has only recently begun to be thoroughly researched, and as a primer, Huby Fairhead's *Decoy Sites*, published by the Norfolk & Suffolk Aviation Museum, is recommended.

This huge complex of fields just south of BARTON BENDISH was used as a Dispersed Landing Ground by 3 Group bombers from 1940-43. When aircraft were not using the site it served as an unofficial daylight K site, utilising wood-and-canvas Wellington mockups. During exercises in 1941 two Army co-operation squadrons - nos. 26 & 268 - were briefly based here, flying Lysanders and Tomahawks. There were plans to develop Barton Bendish as a full-blown bomber airfield, but severe drainage problems led to another site being selected, at Downham Market. Late in the War, US Army liaison aircraft - mainly L4 Grasshoppers - were active at the site.

The heavily overgrown Bunker of the SOUTH ACRE Q site, which served as a decoy for Marham. As far as is known, the site was never attacked.

FULMODESTON served as a decoy for West Raynham (KQ25). This view shows the overgrown Bunker, with the corrugated roof of the partly-buried Ops Room visible. The raised concrete platform would have carried a powerful spotlight.

The entrance to the FULMODESTON Bunker, with the Blast Wall still largely intact. The site was attacked on at least two occasions.

128

A very sophisticated decoy was established at SOUTH PICKENHAM (KQ27), of which this well-preserved underground Bunker was part. The site had its own anti-aircraft guns, which were augmented in times of intense Luftwaffe activity. Some 200 bombs were dropped on the decoy, including a 1,000-pounder that failed to explode.

Interior of the Bunker, showing the arched concrete construction.

Easily viewed from the Nar Valley Way footpath, this is the Control Bunker for the former Q site at WORMEGAY. The earth banking that originally covered the building has worn away, exposing the brick and concrete construction.

Interior of the Control Bunker, looking from the Ops Room through to the Generator Room.

The exposed Q site Bunker at **WORMEGAY**, with the concrete **Generator Room** at left, entrance in the middle, and corrugated iron **Ops Room** at right, complete with lighting platform.

Detail view of the Generator Room, with the 15" exhaust duct clearly visible. To the left is the very basic latrine, located just far enough from the Bunker to be highly awkward in event of an attack.

Old Ghosts - World War I Airfield Sites

This volume has primarily focussed on airfield sites that were either built or had their heyday during World War 2. However, it is important to remember that Norfolk was involved with military aviation from the very beginning, activity being recorded at Snarehill (near Thetford) as early as 1911. A survey of World War 1 aerodromes reveals a list of very different locations: Great Yarmouth was the site of a major seaplane base; Narborough one of the largest training centres in the country; and Pulham a huge airship station. Indeed, during the Great War the County of Norfolk was dotted with airfields and landing sites large and small, though not quite to the extent that prevailed between 1939 and 1945.

In considering World War I airfields the role of 51 (Home Defence) squadron cannot be overstated. This unit, nominally based at Marham, conducted anti-Zeppelin patrols and maintained a network of day and night landing grounds throughout the county. Zeppelin attacks began in 1915 on the East Coast, with King's Lynn among the earliest targets. Even at their peak the raids had little more than nuisance value, and 51 sqn had numerous successes against these lumbering aerial behemoths.

As noted previously, the newly-formed RAF went into immediate decline at the close of hostilities, and the majority of World War 1 sites were abandoned by about 1920. Revisiting these locations is a rather demoralising task; many of the landing grounds were never really developed, and even the major sites have been comprehensively erased, leaving only the subtlest clues to their existence. Research is further clouded by incomplete records from that distant era: confusion surrounds the World War 1 use of Methwold for example, and the very existence of the RNAS site at Ringstead is questioned.

Here then, a brief selection of Great War locations, large and small. These are, quite literally, Ghost Fields.

North Lynn Farm, KING'S LYNN, was briefly used as an airfield during World War 1. Voisin aircraft assembled by the famous Lynn firm of Savage's were test-flown from the site.

Located barely a mile from the World War 2 station at Downham Market, this large field at BEXWELL served as an Emergency Landing Ground in the Great War.

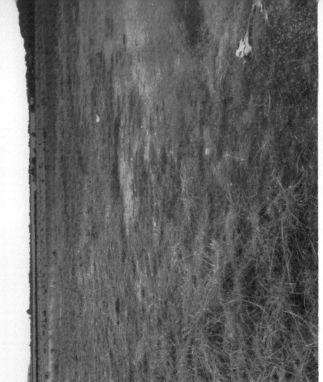

Looking eerily like the plains of West Texas, this is the former World War 1 aerodrome at SEDGEFORD. Originally a Landing Ground for Yarmouth-based Royal Naval Air Service aircraft, it subsequently passed to the Royal Flying Corps and hosted a wide variety of training squadrons. A victim of the post-war contraction of the RAF, the site closed in 1920, but saw use in World War 2 as a decoy for Bircham Newton.

Arguably the most significant World War 1 aerodrome in Norfolk was NARBOROUGH. Originally a RNAS site, the RFC took over the field in April 1916, developing it into a major training station and one of the largest airfields in Britain by 1918. As well as RFC units, American fighter (Pursuit) squadrons and elements of the fledgling Women's Royal Air Force were trained here, but despite its importance Narborough closed in 1920. It fell to the nearby satellite of Marham to become a front-line station by World War 2, and on to the present day. Some of Narborough's buildings survived into the 1980s, but unfortunately no attempt was made to preserve them, and all that remains today is rubble.

Although no buildings remain on-site at Narborough, one of the station's former hangars survives, having been re-erected at TERRINGTON ST CLEMENT. Today the building thrives as an antique and furniture centre, and is well worth a visit.

This unassuming farm track was once the main entrance to the airfield at SEDGEFORD. The ærodrome was used for the formation and training of a variety of bomber and fighter squadrons, many of which later deployed to France and further afield. Sedgeford was eventually eclipsed by nearby Bircham Newton, and did not last long in the RAF era.

Many airfields were conveniently sited near to railway lines, but SEDGEFORD went a stage further, having its own short branch and railhead. Not much remains of this area apart from an embankment and large chunks of rubble. However, elsewhere on the site (see below), some buildings survive, albeit in poor condition.

Few former airfields have been as comprehensively erased as **MOUSEHOLD HEATH**, now obliterated by the Heartsease estate in Norwich. From 1915 to 1918 a number of squadrons were formed and trained at this site, several of them later transferring to the front lines in France. Post-war, Mousehold was home to the famous aircraft manufacturers Boulton & Paul, and later served as Norwich Municipal Airport. In World War 2 it was a K site daylight decoy.

A Landing Ground used by 51 sqn was this site at **TOTTENHILL**. Quarrying began here in the 1930s and continues to this day - some of the hardcore extracted was used to build the runways at Downham Market.

Electricity pylons march across the former airfield site at SPORLE, a Class 3 Night Landing Ground also used by 51 sqn during its anti-Zeppelin operations.

A Class 2 Landing Ground, WEST RUDHAM was another of the sites used by 51 sqn during anti-Zeppelin patrols.